FAMILIES NURTURING FAITH

A Parents' Guide to
the Preschool Years

Leif Kehrwald
and Rene Kehrwald

THE WORLD OF
DON BOSCO
MULTIMEDIA

NEW ROCHELLE, NY

Families Nurturing Faith: A Parents' Guide to the Preschool Years is published as part of the Catholic Families Series—resources to promote faith growth in Families.
Materials available for parish and diocesan leaders, parents and families

Available titles:

For leaders and ministers:
Families and Young Adults
Families and Youth
Families and Young Adolescents
Growing in Faith: A Catholic Family Sourcebook
Media, Faith, and Families: A Parish Ministry Guide
Rituals for Sharing Faith: A Resource for Parish Ministers
Faith and Families: A Parish Program for Parenting in Faith Growth

For parents and families:
Families Sharing Faith: A Parents' Guide to the Grade School Years
Families Experiencing Faith: A Parents' Guide to the Young Adolescent Years
Families Exploring Faith: A Parents' Guide to the Older Adolescent Years
Families Encouraging Faith: A Parents' Guide to the Young Adult Years
Media, Faith, and Families: A Parents' Guide to Family Viewing
Family Rituals and Celebrations

The Catholic Families Series is a publishing project of Don Bosco Multimedia and the Center for Youth Ministry Development

Families Nurturing Faith: A Parents' Guide to the Preschool Years
©1992 Salesian Society, Inc. / Don Bosco Multimedia
475 North Ave., P.O. Box T, New Rochelle, NY 10802

Library of Congress Cataloging-in-Publication Data
Families Nurturing Faith: A Parents' Guide to the Preschool Years /
    Leif and Rene Kehrwald
p. cm. — Catholic Families Series
Includes bibliographical references.
    1. Family life 2. Religious development
        I. Kehrwald, Leif. II. Kehrwald, Rene.
ISBN 0-89944-257-9 $6.95

Design and Typography by Sally Ann Zegarelli, Long Branch, NJ 07740

Printed in the United States of America

6/92   9 8 7 6 5 4 3 2 1

PREFACE

FAMILIES NURTURING FAITH: A PARENTS' GUIDE TO THE PRESCHOOL YEARS

A quick look at the family section of your local bookstore will reveal dozens of books about parenting. What you probably will not find among these titles is a book about parenting and faith growth. To fill this void, we have created five books which help parents of children from the preschool years through the young adult years nurture the faith growth of their children. These new titles are part of the Catholic Families Series published by Don Bosco Multimedia.

Family life changes for all time with the entry of an infant into the family. Rooms get reshuffled and family roles redefined. Change becomes a constant in family life as infants turn to toddlers and toddlers start to run. Important first lessons about love and forgiveness, right and wrong, are passed on verbally and non-verbally, through actions and through words. The child is shaped by his/her family and reshapes the family in return. Part of that shaping and passing on involves sharing an experience of God and faith life with children. What they learn about faith from parents and family in the first few years of their lives provides a strong foundation for all later teaching and experience.

Families Nurturing Faith is specifically designed for parents of preschool children. It provides an understanding of the unique characteristics of preschoolers and their families at this stage of life. It outlines the possibilities for sharing faith with preschool children through the authors' personal stories and through specific strategies and activities. It also suggests ways that you can continue growing yourself as you walk with your child in faith.

Our hope is to promote opportunities for families with preschool children to make a healthy start in sharing the faith story. We hope you find the stories, insights, and ideas a source of support and encouragement in your task of parenting.

ABOUT THE AUTHORS

Leif and Rene Kehrwald reside in Portland, Oregon and are the parents of two boys. Leif serves as Family Life Director for the Archdiocese of Portland. He has published several articles on family life and parish, ministry, including an issue of *Catholic Update*, "Making Family A Priority in Your Parish." He is the author of *Caring That Enables: A Manual for Developing Parish Family Ministry* (Paulist Press), and is co-editor of *Families and Youth: A Resource Manual* (Catholic Families Series.

CONTENTS

1

PARENTING FOR FAITH GROWTH TODAY

WHY FAMILIES NEED FAITH

As every good parent knows, parenting involves much more than providing basic food and shelter, education and health care. Parenting is also about loving and caring, building self-esteem and a sense of values. Effective parenting helps children understand how they relate to others and what they can do to make the world a better place for themselves and for all people.

Parenting is a shared task. Despite all the different shapes that families come in today—single-parent and two-parent, blended and extended—the challenge of parenting continues to be shared across generations and across family lines. Grandparents, aunts and cousins share in the task, as do special friends who have become "family" for us in a different way.

Faith provides family members with shared beliefs and values to guide their life together and to direct their involvement beyond the family circle. Faith values nurture the family's well-being and provide it with the criteria needed to weigh and evaluate the many messages that come its way each day. Faith proclaims, for example, that every person is endowed by God with dignity and blessed with a unique mix of gifts and talents. These gifts and talents, in turn, are meant to be shared with others. This vision of personhood calls families to recognize, nurture and celebrate the uniqueness of each family member. It also calls families to recognize their interdependence with others and to share the talents and gifts nurtured in family life with others in their community and world. As simple as this faith value seems, it often stands in sharp contrast to societal messages that judge people in light of what they have or that promote isolation from others who seem, at least at first glance, to be different from us.

As parents model faith values at home and in the community, nurture a sense of dignity and uniqueness in their children and encourage family members to share their talents with others, they join with God in the sacred task of building a world based on gospel values. Children, in turn, take what they have learned and practiced at home and carry it into the world, guaranteeing a new generation committed to creating a world based on gospel values.

Faith serves, as well, as a source of comfort and strength for parents, assuring them that they are not alone in the task of parenting and providing them with a special Friend to whom they can turn for direction and support. As parents join with their God in the task of parenting, they come to realize that there are no social, geographical or educational barriers to good parenting. Good parenting does not depend upon a high hourly wage, a prestigious address or the number of degrees after a person's name. You don't have to be a biological parent to develop a strong family life. You can be an adoptive parent, a single parent, a parent of healthy or handicapped children. Good parenting is possible for all people who trust enough in themselves, in the other members of their families and in their God.

Faith provides people with the values and vision needed to live life fully. Families need faith to survive and thrive in today's world. Our challenge in this book is to offer you and your family practical insights and strategies for developing a meaningful faith life.

KEYS TO EFFECTIVE PARENTING

Before we begin this book on parenting for faith growth and turn to the descriptions and suggestions offered by our authors, it will be important to look at the adventure of parenting today and what we mean by parenting for faith growth.

As noted above, the key to effective parenting lies within you. Your drive to make your family the best that it can be need not be blocked by your particular life circumstances. To be sure, your path may be more winding and littered than some, but effectiveness in parenting is an internal quality, not easily squashed by external conditions. It is a desire to make the most of yourself and your family, whatever your talents or situation.

What do we know about effective parenting? Who can we turn to for advice? One of the best sources for our wisdom about parenting is to turn to other parents. In *Back to the Family*, Dr. Ray Guarendi gathered the shared wisdom of one hundred of America's happiest and most effective families. He shares the following thoughts on what makes families effective:[1]

1. **A strong home life does not depend upon a parent's education, occupation, ethnicity or social status.** Neither is it limited to biological parents, two-parent homes or a low-stress

existence. Effective parenting and a strong home life are not the product of external causes but are born internally. They evolve from commitment, from determination to build upon your family's strengths, regardless of what factors may be pulling against you.

2.   Successful parents are not all products of successful childhoods. While many parents knew upbringings filled with positive examples from which to anchor their own parenting, others have lived through childhoods best described as cold, abusive or even traumatic. Parents who have risen far above their childhoods are living proof that, contrary to some experts' opinions, the quality of your past does not put a ceiling on the quality of your present as a parent or as a person.

3.   Effective parents are not perfect or even close to perfect. They wrestle with worries, insecurities and guilts all parents feel. They don't have all the answers, endless patience or perfect children. Their lives reveal that skillful parenting is not inborn. It is developed over time, along with a healthy acceptance of one's imperfections. Better parenting results from recognizing our limits and working to overcome them or live with them.

4. Good parents love to parent. They've experienced the challenges and fears inherent to childrearing and remain grateful for the opportunity to be parents. Lifestyles and priorities can change radically with the decision to raise children. Responsible parents accept this reality, even welcome it.

5.   Common sense and good judgment form the foundation for sound parenting decisions. Having discovered that no one right way exists for handling any situation, effective parents strive for self-confidence. It leads to more decisive parenting and more secure children. Childrearing is a never-ending process. It is drawing upon the knowledge and experience of others—children, parents and experts. The willingness to learn from others is indispensable to better parenting, but ultimately you must judge for yourself what will work for your family, based upon your values and unique circumstances.

6.   **A parent's personality has far more influence on her childrearing than being aware of all the latest childrearing trends.** Work to become a better person and your parenting will automatically improve.

7.   **Wise parents are open to guidance from their children.** Children are natural teachers of childrearing. They know us well—in many ways, better than anyone else does. Since they are with us every day, they are ready and able to give us feedback on our technique. Living mirrors, they reflect back at us who we are, what we act like, what we sound like. Lessons most basic to successful parenting are taught by children:

- *Show your love.* At the heart of all quality parenting is unconditional love. No matter what our children do, our love for them will never cease. Unconditional love is the basis for every parenting decision and action. It is the driving force behind all discipline.

- *Teach through example; practice what you preach.*

- *Listen before you talk.*

- *Look through a child's eyes.* Children do not see parenthood through the eyes of parents.

8.   **A relaxed parent is a better parent.** How fully we enjoy our children is directly related to two factors: a relaxed attitude toward childrearing and being prepared for the inevitable rough times that every parent faces. There are ways to parent more calmly right now. Enjoyable childrearing begins with accepting several parenting facts of life. These are truths at the very heart of parenthood.

- *Don't try to be a perfect parent.* Undeserved anxiety and guilt will follow.

- *Don't fear mistakes.* They are necessary for maturation. Good parents become better through mistakes.

- *Parent in the present.* Second guessing yourself or dwelling on the uncertain future will erode your confidence and ability to give your best to your children today.

- *Expect that your children will misunderstand and dislike you at times.* That is a reality of responsible parenthood.

- *Laugh whenever and wherever you can during child-rearing.* Humor helps maintain perspective and eases anxiety.

9. Spiritual beliefs are a dominant presence in strong families. Faith in a Creator and in living by God's guidelines provide values which nurture each member's personal growth and thereby the family's. Spirituality fosters parenting through example, the most durable parenting. It is a source of comfort and strength, enabling parents to call upon a supreme authority for wisdom and direction.

10. There are no shortcuts to strong family life. A parent must invest time. Dedication means a willingness to give quantity time, which is necessary for quality time. Time provides the framework for all elements of family success—communication, discipline, values. Making family a priority fosters a child's self-esteem and sense of belonging. Nothing is more precious to a child than the presence of a parent.

11. Competent parents concentrate on mastering the basics of communication. A few good principles guide them:

- *Talk less at children and listen more to them.* Attentive silence is the simplest way to evoke a child's feelings.

- *Become sensitive to children's prime times to talk.* Arrange them or be present when they occur. They are windows into their thoughts.

- *Affection is continuous communication.* It is love without words. Strong families know the binding power of affection.

■ *Whenever possible, allow children a voice in family decisions.* While in most cases, parents retain the final say, merely being consulted makes a child feel an integral part of the family.

12. Responsible parents expect much of their children and of themselves. Their attitude is, "Success is not measured against others but against yourself. Striving for your personal best is a success." Parents counsel:

■ *Insist on your children's full effort in academics.* It is their future.

■ *The family home is everyone's home, so make it everyone's responsibility,* down to the youngest members.

■ *Judge children's capabilities—social, emotional, personal—and expect them to live up to them.* Don't allow them to live down to the norm.

13. Strong parents believe in strong discipline begun young. They are willing to exert whatever effort is necessary to discipline their children today so life won't discipline them tomorrow. The firmest parent, if loving, is a more gentle teacher than the world. For a child's sake, parents need the will to discipline. The best discipline is motivated by unconditional love, love that is unaffected by a child's misbehavior. Good disciplinarians focus most on what children do right, not wrong. They emphasize the positive. Not only does this make for less discipline, it enhances a child's self image. By their nature, children test limits and want more than is healthy for them. Loving parents are not afraid to say no. They draw clear boundaries within which a child is free to operate.

The mechanics of effective discipline are summarized by the three C's: calm, consistency and consequences. Calm discipline works more quickly and leads to less regrettable behavior from everyone. Consistency is predictability. It enables children to understand and accept the results of their actions. Consequences, not words, are the basic tools of discipline.

14. Strong families rely on simple, clear-cut home rules enforced by consequences. They derive some of their stability from house rules. Established according to a family's needs and goals, rules make for a more content household. The content of the rules changes as the family evolves, but their purpose remains the constant: to promote mutual respect, responsibility and a more pleasant environment for everyone.

Refined to its most basic elements, successful parenting is unconditional love, commitment, teaching by example and the will to discipline. Effective parenting is an attainable reality. Build upon the essentials, and no level of family success is beyond your reach. In this book we will be encouraging you to utilize these ingredients of effective parenting by suggesting practical insights and skills for parenting young adults.

THE FAMILY AS A LIVING SYSTEM

No human being grows in a vacuum. To be human is, by definition, to be interdependent, to rely on others for the support and assistance needed to grow to full life. No place is this more apparent than in the life of the family. Family members depend upon one another and have a tremendous impact on one another's growth. Change and growth in any family member's life automatically impacts all other family members. If a major change occurs in the life of a single family member, all members are forced to adjust to the change. This can entail adjustments in the relationships among individual family members or a recasting of what it means to be family together.

Researchers use the term "system" to describe the organic relationship that exists between individual family members and the family as a whole. You may remember from high school science classes that living organisms and their environments function as a system. All living systems attempt to maintain *equilibrium* or balance. When a change takes place that upsets this balance, the system responds by doing something to restore the equilibrium that existed previously.

The family is a system, too—a system in which relationships change in response to the changing needs and concerns of family members and in response to changes in the family's relationship with the larger society. And like other systems, families attempt to maintain a sense of equilibrium in their relationships. Certain understandings develop regarding roles, rules, relationships and responsibilities in the family. These understandings form the system by which the family operates. Often times, families are unaware of how these roles, rules, relationships and responsibilities affect their entire life as a family.

The tendency for family systems to try to maintain their established patterns of behavior is challenged from time to time by changes to which they must adapt. These changes can be a regular part of the family's growth and development. The birth of the first child causes an imbalance in the family system of the couple, often making many of the former roles, rules, relationships and responsibilities unworkable. The arrival of adolescence brings with it periods of imbalance as formerly accepted roles, rules, relationships and responsibilities are questioned by the adolescent. During these life transitions it is *healthy* for family roles, rules, relationships and responsibilities to change, for through such changes families adjust to the changes and restore a new balance to the system.

Sometimes these changes are brought about by major events in the life of the family, such as the loss of a parent through death or divorce or the remarriage of parents resulting in a new blended family. The members of a family must find ways to reorganize and reestablish workable roles, rules, relationships and responsibilities in light of these major life events. Such changes often result in longer periods of imbalance as the family system seeks to adjust to the changes and establish a new balance. Making changes during these major events is difficult, but it is *healthy*. Families need to adjust to the new situation they face and restore a new balance to the system. Only in this way can the family feel comfortable again.

At other times, you as the parent may wish to make a change in the family by introducing new ways of relating, new patterns of family living, new rules, new practices, etc. In this book we introduce you to a variety of ways to share faith with your children. You may want to use many of these new ideas in your family. Be aware that family members often resist change, not because the changes are bad, but because change is upsetting. It causes anxiety. When a family establishes its balance, members are comfortable with the status quo. Anything new, even if positive, will likely be resisted, and a subtle message of "change back" will be communicated. Change requires at least three steps: the change itself, the family's reaction to the change and dealing with the family's reaction to the change. By understanding how your family system works (what the roles, rules, relationship patterns and responsibilities are), you can be prepared for your family's reaction. For example, you can identify what needs to change in order to introduce the idea, involve family members in deciding and planning for the change, keep communication lines open during the change, suggest that they try the new idea for a specific length of time and then evaluate, etc.

HOW FAMILIES GROW

Today it has become commonplace to talk about the changes we experience throughout our lives. We are aware of the differing life tasks and characteristics of childhood, adolescence, young adulthood, middle adulthood and later adulthood. Each of these "stages" or times of life brings with it new challenges and important life tasks to accomplish. In a family both children and parents are experiencing their own individual journeys.

We may not be as fully aware that the family as a unit or system has important life tasks to address and needs and functions to fulfill. A family in its "infancy" is different from a family in its "adolescence." Like individuals, families move through a life cycle, a family life cycle—that is, various stages in which new issues arise and different concerns predominate. During the first years of marriage, for example, families focus nearly all their energy on establishing a household, finding suitable employment and strengthening the marital relationship. During the child-bearing stage, the family's concerns shift to taking care of their young children. Families are likely to have higher medical expenses, more debts in general and concerns about managing work and family commitments. During the "young adult" stage, when children begin leaving home, families are usually less strained financially, and their concerns shift to reorganizing the household in response to their children's departure. Each stage of the family life cycle is different from those that came before and those that will follow.

These family life cycle changes are a regular part of the family's growth and development. Consequently, in order to understand the changing nature of family relationships throughout the family life cycle, we must take into account not only characteristics of the developing child or adolescent or young adult, but characteristics of the parents and of the family as a system at each stage of life.

A family life cycle perspective sees the family as a three or four generational system moving through time in a life cycle of distinct stages. During each stage the family is confronted with particular tasks to accomplish and challenges to face in order to prepare itself and its members for further growth and development. Viewing family life through a systems perspective can be a powerful tool for helping people understand what is happening in the life of their family and for creating strategies that promote individual and family faith growth and sharing.

Starting with the new couple, the following brief paragraphs describe the tasks faced by families at each stage of development. While no single development theory can explain all the factors that contribute to individual and family growth, such theories do provide windows through which we can gain a better understanding of how families change and grow. They help us understand what is happening in the life of the individual and in the life of the family as a whole.[2]

NEW COUPLE

Marriage joins not just two individuals, but two families together in a new relationship. It presents the new couple with a series of new challenges, including:

- defining and learning the role of husband and wife;

- establishing new relationships as a couple with their families of origin and with their friends;

- developing a commitment to a new family, with its own rules, roles, responsibilities, values and traditions.

As they confront these challenges, the new couple often finds themselves reflecting on the influence of their family of origin to draw insights, values and traditions that they want to include in their new family. This reflection helps them to sort out emotionally what they will take along from the family of origin, what they will leave behind and what they will create for themselves.

FAMILIES WITH CHILDREN

With the birth of the first child, the couple embarks on a new life task—to accept new members into the family and to adjust the rules, roles, responsibilities and relationships of their family to include the needs of the youngest members. The challenge for families with children involves:

- developing parenting roles and skills;

- negotiating and joining in childrearing, financial and household tasks;

- realigning relationships with extended family to include grandparenting roles;

- sharing socialization with the outside world;

- developing new patterns of family communication, traditions, celebrations.

FAMILIES WITH ADOLESCENTS

Adolescence ushers in a new era in family life brought on by new adolescent life tasks and the changing role of the parents in relationship to their adolescent children. The changes of adolescence—puberty, new ways of thinking, wider sphere of social activity and relationships, greater autonomy—present the family as a whole with a new set of challenges. In fact, it would be fair to say that the whole family experiences adolescence. The challenge for families with adolescents involves:

- allowing for the increasing independence of adolescents, while maintaining enough structure to foster continued family development;

- reflection by adult members on their personal, marital and career life issues;

- adjusting patterns of family communication, traditions, celebrations;

- and for some families beginning the shift toward joint caring for the older generation.

The task for most families with adolescents—and it is by no means an easy one—is to maintain *emotional* involvement, in the form of concern and caring, while gradually moving toward a relationship characterized by greater *behavioral* autonomy.

FAMILIES WITH YOUNG ADULTS

The most significant aspect of this stage of life is that it is marked by the greatest number of exits and entries of family members. The stage begins with the launching of grown children into schooling, careers and homes of their own, and proceeds with the entry of their spouses and children. The challenge for families with young adults involves:

- regrouping as a family as each young adult moves out from the family;

- changes in the marital relationship now that parenting responsibilities are no longer required;

- development of adult-to-adult relationships between grown children and their parents;

- realigning relationships to include in-laws and grand-children;

- caring for the older generation and dealing with disabilities and death.

This stage of family life also presents unique challenges to the young adult, for example:

- accepting emotional and financial responsibility for oneself;

- formulating personal life goals;

- developing intimate peer relationships;

- establishing oneself in the world of work.

FAMILIES IN LATER LIFE

Among the tasks of families in later life is the adjustment to retirement, which not only may create the obvious vacuum for the retiring person, but may put a special strain on the marriage. Financial insecurity and dependence are also special difficulties, especially for family members who value managing for themselves. And while loss of friends and relatives is a particular difficulty at this phase, the loss of a spouse is the most difficult adjustment, with its problems of reorganizing one's entire life alone after many years as a couple and of having fewer relationships to help replace the loss. Grandparenthood can, however, offer a new lease on life and opportunities for special close relationships without the responsibilities of parenthood.

In this book we will describe many of the major characteristics and concerns of the growing child, as well as those of parents and the family as a whole. These explanations will help you to understand the changing nature of family relationships during early childhood and to offer practical suggestions for parenting and faith growth in families with young children.

HOW FAMILIES GROW IN FAITH

The Christian vision of family life speaks about the family as a community of life and love. It proclaims that family life is sacred and that family activities are holy, that God's love is revealed and communicated in new ways each and every day through Christian families. This Christian vision of family life calls families to a unique identity and mission. This means that the Christian family has several important responsibilities as it seeks to grow in faith:

- *Families form a loving community.*
  Families work to build a community based on love, compassion, respect, forgiveness and service to others. In families, people learn how to give and receive love and how to contribute to the good of other family members. In families, people open themselves to experiencing God's love through their dealings with one another, through the ethnic and cultural values and traditions that are part of family life and through the events of family life.

- *Families serve life by bearing and educating children.*
  Families serve life by bringing children into the world, by handing on Catholic Christian values and traditions and by developing the potential of each member at every age. As parents and all family members share their values with one another, they grow toward moral and spiritual maturity.

- *Families participate in building a caring and just society.*
  Families participate in building a caring and just society.

The gospel values of service, compassion and justice are first learned and practiced in families. In Christian families people learn how to reach out beyond the home to serve those in need and to work for justice for all God's people. How family members learn to relate to each other with respect, love, caring, fidelity, honesty and commitment becomes their way of relating to others in the world.

■   *Families share in the life and mission of the Church.*
Families share in the life and mission of the Church when the gospel vision and values are communicated and applied in daily life, when faith is celebrated through family rituals or through participation in the sacramental life of the church, when people gather as a family or parish community to pray, when people reach out, in Jesus' name, in loving service to others.

These responsibilities may sound overwhelming and unrealistic given all your other responsibilities as parents. In this book we will use these four responsibilities to develop practical ideas that you can use to share faith and promote individual and family faith growth. We will organize our ideas around six time-honored ways of sharing faith: (1) sharing the Catholic faith story, (2) celebrating faith through rituals, (3) praying together, (4) enriching family relationships, (5) responding to those in need through actions of justice and service, and (6) relating to the wider community.

Sharing the Catholic faith story happens when parents share stories from the Scriptures with their children, when families discuss the implications and applications of Christian faith for daily living, when a moral dilemma is encountered and the family turns to the resources of the Catholic faith for guidance, when parents discuss the religious questions their children ask. The family's sharing is complemented by participation of children, parents and/or the entire family in the catechetical program of the parish community.

Celebrating faith through rituals happens when the family celebrates the liturgical year, such as Advent and

Christmas, Lent and Easter; celebrates the civic calendar, like Martin Luther King, Jr. Day and Earth Day; celebrates milestones or rites of passages, such as birthdays, anniversaries, graduations, special recognitions; celebrates ethnic traditions which have been passed down through the generations; celebrates the rituals of daily life, like meal prayer and forgiveness. These celebrations provide the foundations for a family ritual life in which God is discovered and celebrated through the day, week, month and year. The family's ritual life is complemented by participation in the ritual life of the parish community with its weekly celebration of the Eucharist; regular sacramental celebrations, such as Reconciliation and Anointing of the Sick; and liturgical year celebrations.

Praying together as a family is a reality when families incorporate prayer into the daily living through meal and bed times, times of thanksgiving and of crisis; when parents teach basic prayers and pray with their children. The family's prayer life is complemented by participation in the communal prayer life of the parish community, especially through liturgical year celebrations.

Enriching family relationships occurs when the family spends both quality and quantity time together; participates in family activities; works at developing healthy communication patterns which cultivate appreciation, respect and support for each other; negotiates and resolves problems and differences in positive and constructive ways. Enriching family relationships also involves the parents in developing their marriage relationship or a single parent developing intimate, supportive relationships in his or her life.

Performing acts of justice and service takes place when the family recognizes the needs of others in our communities and in our world and seeks to respond. Families act through stewardship and care for the earth; through direct service to others, the homeless and the hungry; through study of social issues; through developing a family lifestyle based on equality, nonviolence, respect for human dignity, respect for the earth. The family's service involvement is strengthened when it is done together with other families in the parish community.

Relating as a family to the wider community happens when families join together in family support groups or family clusters for sharing, activities and encouragement; when families learn about the broader church and world, especially the cultural heritages of others in the community or the world; when families organize to address common concerns facing them in the community, like quality education or safe neighborhoods.

This is quite a challenge for the family! Don't be overwhelmed. What is essential is that you identify how you already share faith using these six ways and try new approaches that will enrich your family life. In this book we have included ideas to support your current efforts and to encourage you to try new ways to share faith. Adapt and revise these ideas so that they work for you.

Remember that the family shares responsibility with the parish community for promoting faith growth in each of these six ways. A careful look at the six ways will reveal the basic functions of the parish community, e.g., religious education, sacraments and worship, serving the needs of others. The parish and family approach each of these six ways of sharing faith differently. The parish community needs to support and encourage the efforts of families to share faith. Families need to be involved in the life of the parish community so that their family efforts can be connected to the larger community of faith. Don't be afraid to challenge your parish community and its leaders to support families and to offer programs and services for families that will promote the family's growth in faith.

GROWING TOWARD MATURITY IN FAITH

What do we hope will happen in the lives of family members—parents and children alike—if we strengthen our efforts at sharing faith? It is our hope that family members will discover meaning and purpose for their lives in a life-transforming relationship with a loving God in Jesus Christ and a consistent devotion to serving others as Jesus did.

Our growth as Catholic Christians is never complete. It is a life-long journey towards greater maturity in faith. While no complete description of this journey is possible, we hope and pray that you and your family will grow toward a living faith characterized by the following elements:

- trusting in God's saving grace and firmly believing in the humanity and divinity of Jesus Christ;

- experiencing a sense of personal well-being, security and peace;

- integrating faith and life—seeing work, family, social relationships and political choices as part of your religious life;

- seeking spiritual growth through Scripture, study, reflection, prayer and discussion with others;

- seeking to be part of a Catholic community of believers in which people give witness to their faith, support and nourish one another, serve the needs of each other and the community, and worship together;

- developing a deeper understanding of the Catholic Christian tradition and its applicability to life in today's complex society;

- holding life-affirming gospel values, including respect for human dignity, commitment to uphold human rights, equality (especially racial and gender), stewardship, care and compassion and a personal sense of responsibility for the welfare of others;

- advocating for social and global change to bring about greater social justice and peace;

- serving humanity, consistently and passionately, through acts of love and justice.

Families provide a natural context for nurturing God's gift of faith. As families and individuals grow together in faith, life is enriched and the gospel vision brought closer to reality. Faith and family are a natural duo. May this volume be one small step toward helping you grow together more effectively.

End Notes

[1] These points about effective parenting were summarized from *Back to the Family* by Ray Guarendi (New York: Villard Books, 1990).

[2] The family life cycle perspective described below was adapted from "The Family Life Cycle," by Betty Carter and Monica McGoldrick in *Growing in Faith: A Catholic Family Sourcebook,* ed. John Roberto (New Rochelle: Don Bosco Multimedia, 1990.)

2

UNDERSTANDING FAMILIES WITH PRESCHOOL CHILDREN

Becoming a family with children is one of the most dramatic changes we experience as adults. Most of us never realized how having a baby could change our entire lives—forever. The physical, emotional and social responsibilities that come with parenting can be overwhelming, especially at the beginning. This chapter will explore some of the typical needs, struggles, challenges and joys of families with young children. We will look at specific issues for parents, as well as the growth issues for young children, and then put them together for a "holistic" view of families with young children.

LIFE TASKS FOR PARENTS

When two people get married, they pledge themselves to each other in love. In a healthy marriage this does not mean they give up being themselves but begin to share a life together.

While marriage calls for a mutual giving of self, parenting, at least at initially, demands a complete giving of self to a person who can give little or nothing in return. One of the most challenging Christian virtues is to give without expecting anything in return; to love *unconditionally*. This is exactly the task parents must embrace when their first child enters the world.

We marvel at the miraculous creation of new life when a child is born. We give thanks to God for allowing us to participate in creating a new human person. It is truly a miracle. Yet, another miracle occurs as God gives us the courage, strength, endurance and love to care for and nurture this new life. Psychologists call this "generativity:" the ability to give so much of oneself to another that the other person is empowered to truly live. In the act of parenting, we mirror God's "generativity" with all people.

Parents of young children, ages newborn to four, know the meaning of generativity in its most basic form. Our lives are suddenly not our own, and it is difficult to share time, space, sleep, possessions, even the bathroom with our children.

Yet God is still there. When our children were infants, we often wondered how single parents survived; working together, we were stretched to the breaking point! Each day we toiled from the moment our baby woke us until we collapsed in bed, only to be awakened in the middle of the night. How could someone so little cause such a flurry of activity and keep it up for so long with so little sleep? For months, we felt like we were just surviving.

In the midst of all this giving, young parents must seek ways to **replenish** themselves, the corresponding task of generativity. If we just give and give and give, the well will run dry and we risk losing part of our personhood.

Replenishment means making time (especially when you don't feel that you have any) for your own personal growth.

While your child grows and develops, so must you. Although your time and energy are limited, finding new ways to play, relax and exercise are very important. Take a class, resume an old hobby, walk regularly with a friend or do anything that will rejuvenate your mind, heart and body. Your whole family will benefit because you'll have more patience and energy to meet the constant demands of your little one(s).

Replenishment also means remembering to whom you are married and respecting and nurturing the primacy of that relationship, so that it can continue to strengthen and inspire you. This may mean committing to a once a week date, no matter what, or to a brief evening prayer each night before collapsing into bed. It may mean planning a weekend away from the kids, the house and your jobs just to focus on each other. There is truth to the saying, "The best thing parents can do for their children is love each other." This is also true for single parents who are challenged to develop intimate relationships and supportive communities that strengthen and inspire them.

Replenishment also means seeking support and advice. This may sound logical, but most Americans have been raised to pride themselves on their independence, so the thought of seeking help is a sign of weakness and inadequacy. Yet knowing when and where to seek help is a family strength to be treasured. It's a myth that healthy families never need help.

Seeking support might involve joining a parent support group with others who have young children or starting one if none is available in your area. It might involve taking parenting classes and seminars or perhaps just reading helpful material. (The fact that you have read this far in this book shows you understand the need for replenishment.) It might also mean seeing a counselor or psychologist, if you have questions, to help you determine if your child's behavior is appropriate or if you might need help with some of the many difficult situations parents face. Replenishment is not a sign of weakness but a necessity for parents.

If we do not replenish ourselves it normally doesn't take long for symptoms of parent burnout to surface: excessive fatigue, chronic ill health, irritability. No one appreciates a "martyr" who performs his responsibilities grim-faced, with a lack of joy; it is also not a good model for our children.

Some parents may not have trouble until later in life, perhaps when young adult children are leaving home. If they have not made time to pursue their own interests, they may have trouble letting their children go because too much of their own identity is wrapped up in them. They are afraid that if their children leave there will be nothing left of them. This is not a healthy model either.

Making room for a new child in the family is no small task. The first child is the greatest challenge because he or she launches the whole family into a new stage from which there is no turning back but each successive child also impacts the family dynamics in a unique way.

Becoming a family with young children means renegotiating family boundaries. Relationships between husband and wife and with friends, siblings and extended family are altered. It is not unusual for the father to feel left out of the intimacy shared between a nursing mother and their child, but in just a few years the tables may turn and mom may feel left out when their toddler enjoys playing rambunctiously with dad.

Have you ever noticed how much your conversations are monopolized by talking about your children? And even when you are not, chances are one or both of you is worried about at least one of them! That is why it is so important to be sure that the "new boundaries" include time for just the two of you. Another reason is that as your children get older, your entire conversational pattern may change to incorporate a child's request every thirty seconds. Some parents have acquired great skill in communicating in staccato—short, forceful intervals so that they won't get caught mid-thought by a child's desperate request for a drink of water or to have his bottom wiped. One problem with this communication method is that it may become a habit, and you may use it even when children are not present. You always know when you're talking to a parent who is used to being interrupted!

In single parent families where there isn't someone regularly present to provide a brief respite from children's demands or to share the daily tasks of childrearing, the need for quality personal time with other adults can be especially important. Regular contact with others we respect and trust provides perspective and confirms that we are much more just the roles we are playing at the moment.

Adding children to the family also has an impact on parents' careers. Mother's career will be interrupted for at least a few months, and perhaps as much as a decade, which can be frustrating if she views these as her most productive working years. If she goes back to work, both parents need to grapple with the difficult problem of finding affordable quality childcare. Dad may feel frustrated by increased work demands taking him away from their young and growing family. When both parents are employed, they must juggle their schedules caring for a sick child, meeting doctors' appointments, picking up at preschool, etc. As difficult as these issues may be in two parent families, they can be even more troublesome in single parent families and in situations where taking time off from work just is not an option. The presence of a supportive, extended family in the area can sometimes make such situations easier to handle.

All the child development experts stress that the first three or four years of life are clearly the most formative and important. The rate of growth and learning for the young child is phenomenal compared to the typical growth and learning of an adult. It's no wonder we feel frightened and inadequate as parents when we're told how important this time is for our children.

Suddenly hundreds of questions surface: How can I possibly be a good enough parent? Will my children have faith? Will they be as smart as their peers? Will they get along with their siblings? There's a lot of anxiety and insecurity that goes with parenting, but it is important for parents to feel secure in their parenthood.

Many parents have been seduced into thinking that good parenting simply involves following a standard set of directions that apply to all children. When our children do not respond like the text book says, we feel guilty for not following the steps quite right.

But we have found that raising children is a creative endeavor, an art rather than a science. The "rules" of growth and maturity are not hard and fast, and so parents must rely on their instincts first and foremost. "Expert" advice is helpful as long as you keep your children's personalities and your family "style" in mind, and adapt it to suit your needs and life situation. There is no single right way to parent. What is "right" in a homogeneous suburban setting can be quite different from what is right for city dwellers surrounded by extended family members. A key life task for parents of young children is dealing with the many confidence questions that arise each day, but as you gain more experience and learn to trust that you know what is best for your child, it becomes easier.

LIFE TASKS FOR YOUNG CHILDREN

Understanding child development helps parents appreciate the patterns of their child's growth in all areas: thinking, reasoning, trusting, decision making, loving and faith growth. A child's growth in these areas is intricate, gradual and influenced by numerous factors, including their personality, the emotional atmosphere of the home, the explicit (as well as unspoken) messages from parents and other family members, interactions with peers and siblings and the interdependence of these growth areas.

Let's begin by looking at young children from a parent's perspective, with a little humor. Over the years we have developed our own theories about each stage of development.

Infants. Every possible human need must be provided for children until they learn their first word which will certainly be "NO!" Then children still will require every possible human need, but will want exactly the opposite.

■ The smaller the baby, the more paraphernalia needed to travel. A corollary to this axiom is: the smaller the baby, the bigger the paraphernalia needed (e.g., play-pen, high chair, crib.). A week's vacation at Grandma's requires a U-Haul rental truck!

Toddlers. Children this age cannot register the word "Don't." In fact, they will always do the opposite of what you "don't" want them to do. (Hint: Always word requests in a positive way. "Please step around the mud puddle" has a much better chance of working than, "Don't step in the mud puddle!")

- There's nothing like a parent to bring out the worst in a child, especially in public. Toddlers have a tremendous capacity for high-decibel and very dramatic tantrum-throwing, which typically occurs in the grocery store, but can strike any crowded public place where you are likely to run into someone you know.

Pre-Schoolers. These little people are always happy to tell you what color things are, but when it comes to matching their clothes for school in the morning, suddenly they are color blind.

- Although the frequency and intensity of tantrums have probably subsided, the child's amazing ability to whhhiiiiine becomes more pronounced. We have considered giving our five-year-old voice lessons to teach him the lower end of the scale.

These axioms may not fully describe your child, but we are confident we have named several common, perhaps even core, experiences you may have had with him or her. Newborn to four-year-old children have a great deal of importance and control in the family. Furthermore, through centuries of generational learning, they have adapted and honed their skills, so they not only survive among the BIG PEOPLE, but try to control them at all times!

Kidding aside, several fundamental beliefs about early child development are worth noting here:

- What happens in our earliest years has a fundamental effect on everything we experience after that. We love because we were first loved, or fail to love because we were not loved early in our lives.

- The way we were treated as small children is the way we will treat ourselves and others the rest of our lives: with tenderness and support, with neglect and cruelty or with something in between.

- Each person is precious and worthy of infinite tenderness and support. No place is this more obvious than in the life of a young child.

- The central fear of early childhood is abandonment, of not experiencing the unconditional love from parents and family that is so essential to healthy emotional development.

- Children are exceptionally sensitive but also very resilient and this can create problems. We bounce back from early hurts, and on the surface may appear to have recovered. But we may also have emotionally stayed at the "scene of the crime," and depending upon how deep the wound, we may repeat it again with our own children.

- Our degree of openness to relationships is established in the first four years of life but can be changed or affected by friends, teachers, counselors and other people we may meet.

- Nurturing is an ongoing process, a task of both men and women. The ultimate goal of "good enough parenting" is to make your child feel confident-to-the-core, to feel "I am good and lovable just the way I am."

- Babies are totally dependent and need to be hugged, loved and fed. Gradually, on their own time table, they will initiate their independence. When they learn to separate from you, they will need you to be actively available when needed and in the background to fall back on when not.

■ There can be no more fundamental priority than raising children in a healthy way. The way we hold our children is the way we hold our future.

THE FAMILY WITH YOUNG CHILDREN

What is the ideal family? TV sitcoms might have you believe that it's a successful, two-career family that has no problems, perfectly-behaved, neat children and a lovely home with no leaky faucets. The children never throw tantrums or tease their siblings, the parents have a great sex life, and, of course, they always have time to be involved in school, town and church activities.

The above description hardly fits the majority of (or probably any) young families, though, and life might be pretty dull if it did. In reality, it's quite a balancing act to juggle all of our roles: career, marriage, personal life and parenting. Let's look at some of these challenges.

The pulls between work and home...for both parents. For many, the world of work is not just a major responsibility but also a major source of personal satisfaction and self-esteem. If you have ever been unemployed, you know first hand how your work contributes to your sense of self-worth. For parents this means a struggle between their jobs and the tasks of parenting. Mothers *and* fathers have to balance time at home with a newborn and the demands of returning to work. Mothers *and* fathers have to balance time parenting and caring for children with the demands and satisfaction that their jobs provide them. This balancing act can be difficult in single parent homes and in families where both parents are present, but parenting and household tasks are not equally shared.

Don't forget your marriage. It's common for husbands and wives to neglect their own relationship for the sake of their careers and their children. But to make everything else work, the marriage relationship must be held as a top priority.

Granted, raising children and maintaining careers takes a lot of time at this stage, but we also need the nurturing we get from our spouse and "best friend."

Spending time together is very important. There may have been a time when the two of you naturally spent lots of quality time together. But with the demands of job and children, that time doesn't come automatically any more, at least not very often. If your calendar fills up like most folks, then you know you have to actually carve time from a thousand other pressing responsibilities.

We have friends who do this by maintaining a standing Saturday night date. The "entertainment" column in their family budget is higher than ours, but they know they need the time together. Their three children are really the beneficiaries because those Saturday nights make mom and dad better parents the rest of the week.

We have experimented with different times of the day to be together. We enjoy going out for the evening, but often we are both so tired that our time together is not as much fun as it could be. Because we both have some flexibility in our jobs, we have found mornings together while the children are in preschool to be our best option, and we marvel at how nice it is to be together at the beginning of the day when we are still fresh. Regardless of when, it's important to make out time to re-connect and re-charge each other's batteries.

Single parents likewise need to have their batteries re-charged through regular contact with others who are special in their lives. At times the need may be to talk with someone about what's happening in family life and how it can best be handled. At other times the most pressing need may be just to have someone to relax and joke with. Guaranteeing a minimum of quality time for ourselves is an important requisite for sharing quality family time with young children.

Raising children and sexual equality. Before we had children, all of our households tasks were divided equally. When our first son was born and Rene stayed home to care for him, it was the first time in our married life that only one of us was working outside the home. When, as a result, Leif found himself thinking his new job duties were more important than sharing household tasks, we entered into "serious dialogue" about that attitude. It is not an issue we've been able to settle with just one conversation but a constant source of discussion and attitude adjustment.

Even though our society touts sexual equality, women most often carry the lion's share of household and child-rearing responsibilities, whether they are employed full-time, part-time or at home. There remains in our society a clear, deeply-rooted, sexual distinction between the responsibility for raising children and that of making money.

In spite of this, we are trying to raise our children in an atmosphere of sexual equality, and yet we recognize the strong societal pressure to fall dutifully into the roles described above. Outwardly, it may appear as though we have done just that, but we have made many attempts to counterbalance our "traditional" situation. Leif spends less time at home than does Rene, but few household tasks are reserved strictly for one or the other of us; we just do whatever needs to be done.

When it comes to parenting and nurturing our children, we have been as equal as we can be. Rene does not defer discipline "until your dad gets home;" Leif bathes and dresses the children as well as Rene. But our children turn to us each for different needs. They know they don't have "wrestle time" with mom, and they know dad does not like to fingerpaint, but we believe these are more a reflection of our personality differences than stereotypical differences. We hope our children will grow up with few sexual stereotypes.

Making "space" for children in our lives. Choosing to parent involves consciously making space and time in our lives for a child. Children need regular, quality time from parents and from other adults who share the childrearing task with them. How this is worked out in practice in families can differ greatly. Parenting roles will vary depending on individual talents and abilities, likes and dislikes. Family economics, structure and ethnic background can likewise effect how parenting is carried out. But the need for quality time, freely given and reflecting a unique, loving relationship with the child is essential.

Intimacy and sex. We have already mentioned, facetiously, that the sex life of parents with young children in the ideal family is great. In reality however, the threat of too little time and too many things to worry about for both partners makes sexual intimacy a greater challenge at this stage than perhaps any other. Let's face it, if you *know* you'll be up with a crying baby in a few short hours, there's only one thing on your mind...sleep.

Good sexual intimacy must reflect (and celebrate) the lived experience of the two of you and your family. Sharing the experience of diapers, preschool projects and messy rooms may be a bit tedious, but also sharing your child's joys, struggles and amazingly cute remarks can be a source of satisfaction, joy and intimacy.

Like all areas of married life, sexual intimacy calls for frequent honest sharing and real listening. Give each other permission to talk about your desires and expectations without always having to act on them. Keep in mind, too, that it's normal and healthy for a couple's sexual sharing to change and evolve over time. If these evolutions are never discussed, though, resentments can easily build.

Finding the right time to talk about such a sensitive subject as sex can be a challenge but it is important, because as difficult as it may be, ignoring the problem won't make it go away. You'll probably have more success away from the chaos of your home. We have our most meaningful conversations when we meet after work or take a long walk along the river. We also greatly enjoy an annual overnight at a bed and breakfast inn.

More to intimacy than SEX. Real intimacy encompasses far more than sex. It touches the core of your relationship as friends, lovers, partners, parents and much more. It is giving and receiving; accepting each other as we are at any given moment.

We have had to work hard over the years giving each other permission to feel differently and have contrary emotions. When we are lucky enough to get a whole day together or perhaps even a weekend, one of us invariably starts off in a crummy mood, due to whatever chaos we're leaving behind. Years ago this put a damper on our time together. Now, we simply say to each other, "Be what you need to be. Feel what you need to feel. I accept you." With acceptance, instead of denial, the mood usually fades quickly.

Studies show that marital satisfaction sometimes declines when children are born. Opportunities for private time are greatly reduced, and preoccupation with children and other matters increases. However, the couples who establish solid patterns of sharing intimacy (not just sex) before they have children are more capable of maintaining it when their children are born, so they experience less dissatisfaction.

A marriage that has developed intimacy is better able to respond to the challenge of parenthood and integrate the lifelong change that parenthood brings, not only to the new parents but to the entire family.

Encountering extended family. For some young families, grandparents provide great joy for the children and a tremendous support for parents; for others, the situation is not quite so ideal. The last thing you want to hear from your mother-in-law, as you rinse out another dirty diaper, is how young her children were when they were potty-trained. Different parenting styles and lack of clear communication can cause problems between the generations.

We have experienced both joy and frustration in our nine years of parenting. Our extended family helped a great deal with its care, concern and prayers during two difficult pregnances. At other times, their lack of understanding and sensitivity has caused tension.

Extended family is often a stabilizing force for single parent families.

Our children don't fight with each other, do yours? Actually, that's not completely true; our two lovable, kind and wonderful boys never fight with each other more than *eight* times a day.

What do the experts say about sibling rivalry? They seem to think the issues lie more with us than the children. Experts tell us to examine our relationship with our spouse, which is a model for our children, and how available we are to our children. Often we may, unknowingly, encourage our children to compete with each other for our time and attention. When disciplining, for instance, a common error is to hold one child, rather than all of them, accountable for working things out. Children will be more cooperative when they know they all have to face the same consequences. On the other hand, we may be making a mistake by trying to create an egalitarian family atmosphere because that's not what children will experience out in the world.

It's challenging for us to internalize this advice and act on it. As we write these words, our older child is terrorizing his younger brother. On the surface, it seems hard to imagine giving them both the same consequence: Clearly there is a culprit who deserves discipline and a victim who deserves our sympathy. On the other hand, doesn't the younger one often goad the elder into terrorism just so he can be a victim and run to mom or dad for sympathy? Maybe the experts are right.

CONCLUSION

This stage of family life is tedious and joyous, exhausting and exhilarating, all at the same time. Our young children may appear unassuming, but their impact on our lives, our marriages and our spirits has a greater magnitude than any of us could have imagined during that blissful period when they were just a "twinkle in our eyes."

This stage of family life is key because during this time we transmit our love and faith in God from one generation to the next. When the time is right and God is felt among us, we transmit the true richness of faith to our children and together we catch glimpses of God's creative love.

3

PARENTING SKILLS
FOR FAITH GROWTH

Our boys have been going through a phase we call "passive irresponsibility." Whenever anything bad occurs, it just "happens," but nobody knows who is responsible or why it happened. They have become experts in using the passive voice in their language.

We were keyed into this stage one morning while putting breakfast on the table. Not unexpectedly, Luke spilled his juice. Leif, using his best 6:45 AM parenting skills, responded with an annoyed, "LUUUUUKKE!!!" Luke responded with complete sincerity, "But Dad, I was just sitting here." We suddenly realized that, from his point of view, he was telling the truth; he had no idea what his arms and legs were doing. It's just a phase though, right?

35

It's these "phases" that make parenting so hard. If not "passive irresponsibility," then it will be something else. In fact, we wonder if parenting gets harder with every generation. At least it seems there has never been a generation as hard to parent as the current one, because all we hear from our parents and relatives is what good babies we were, and how early they potty-trained us, and how well we ate string beans, etc.

We are faced with different challenges, though. Life is not as simple. We don't think our parents ever thought about such things as *parenting for faith growth*," let alone read a book about it. With tools such as this, we hope we can rise to the challenge, respond wisely and perhaps create a better generation of children than has ever existed before.

All kidding aside, we strongly believe parenting for faith growth must be a key component for our generation of children. In this chapter, we will expose and dispel several myths about parenting young children and then suggest ten key beliefs and techniques for successful parenting.

Just one note about this chapter. If you are like us, you may, as a couple, not agree on what is good parenting advice. When we have read and discussed parenting material, one of us usually thinks it is *the* answer, while the other doesn't. Or, worse, we may think, "Well, it may work in some homes, but not ours." As you read this chapter, be sure to adapt our suggestions to what works in your family.

INTRODUCTORY THOUGHTS ABOUT PARENTING

How do we know if we're good parents? Is it good enough that we buy them only educational toys and let them watch only educational TV? Is it good enough that we never spank our children and give them as much positive reinforcement as possible? Is it good enough that we remember to slice their hot dogs length-wise and feed them only smooth peanut butter, so they don't choke? The answer to all these questions is maybe yes, maybe no.

As we said in the first chapter, parenting is more art than science. It is more instinct than a set of "how to's." When we blindly follow the instructions of experts the end result can only be frustration. We feel guilty when we try out a technique on our child that "fails," but we shouldn't. WE are not predictable like machinery, and neither are our children.

Parenting is intensely connected to our identity, so its actions are a form of our own self-expression. Children benefit from parents and other adults who are in touch with themselves and communicate not just confidence, but an inner security with life and the world that can never be learned in a parenting book. This strong sense of identity empowers children to cope with life the same way. They begin to think for themselves and learn to handle situations when no specific steps or solutions have been dictated. They are becoming whole people in the fullest sense of the word.

PARENTING FOR FAITH GROWTH

Everything mentioned above is consistent with our Catholic Christian faith. The principles of parenting easily translate to sharing faith with our children. Faith formation, like parenting, is much more than just a set of steps. It truly is an art to create the right atmosphere for a child to catch a glimpse of God's activity and respond to it, because not only is the right atmosphere different for every child in every family, but for every occasion, as well. There can never be a universally prescribed set of steps for sharing faith with our children.

For faith to be lived and real it must connect strongly with life's experiences. We must take advantage of the teachable moments that occur each day in the bathtub, at the dinner table and even in front of the TV. When we recognize God's activity in our children, we try to point it out to them. Unless we're aware of God's presence in our own lives, though, we'll have much more difficulty seeing him in theirs. An artist has a good eye and a strong intuitive sense of what lies beneath the surface of the canvas. Like artists, we can reveal the beauty of God's love that often lies just beneath the surface.

Are we doing enough to share faith with our young children? The Bible stories we share, the rituals we celebrate, the ways we pray together and the ways we serve other people must be connected to lives rooted in faith if they are to bear fruit. To the extent that our faith is lived and real, it will rub off on our children. When we are in touch with our own faith, our teaching and actions will come across with conviction because there is genuine depth and richness to them and they are a natural part of our lives.

Few parents know all the right answers to their children's faith questions, much less how to give them answers they can understand. We certainly don't. Our five-year-old asks repeatedly about the origins of God. "Someone or something must have created God. Who existed before God?" he asks. We have tried to explain that God has always been, but no matter how we say it, he still maintains something or someone must have created God, "In the beginning..." Maybe this is the beginning of a lifetime of theological discussions!

We need to use our unique rapport with our children to communicate the Catholic Christian faith by knowing our faith tradition *and* feeling comfortable dealing with faith questions. Both are important skills for us to develop.

Are we doing enough to help our children develop a personal relationship with God? Every person experiences God in their own way, but as parents we can create an atmosphere for our child to discover and respond to God's activity. If we try to force it, our attempts will probably be rejected (if not now, perhaps later), so our children must be free to discover God in their own way. An important part of that freedom is affirming their experiences when they tell us about them. Our younger son announced, at age four, that he had heard God speak to him. Rene responded by listing several ways that God frequently "speaks" to people: through another's good deed, in a beautiful sunset, in a thought we have while praying, at Sunday Mass. But Luke responded, "No Mom, God used his voice and spoke to me!" Rene had the wisdom to ask what God said. "God told me he loves me and everyone in our family," he said, and then wandered off. It was so matter-of-fact for him that who were we to argue? Regardless of what actually happened, it was a genuine experience of God for him, and Rene could very well have squashed the whole thing. Parenting for faith growth means having a sense of confidence in your relationships with your loved ones.

TWO MYTHS ABOUT PARENTING YOUNG CHILDREN

Every stage of family life has its own particular characteristics and quirks, and each can be distinguished by certain behaviors and qualities. When they become exaggerated, though, like the "terrible two's," they take on mythical qualities. These myths help us distinguish between the stages but can be detrimental if the negative overtones become a self-fulfilling prophecy.

Adolescence is probably most noted for its myths, but following close behind is our stage: young children. We want to expose two myths and cut them down to size. Our parenting challenges are hard enough without a whole set of unspoken expectations that we may accept as truth without examining them.

MYTH #1: PARENTING COMES NATURALLY

Generations ago, young girls were given the impression that their "mothering" talents would naturally emerge when they began having children. And in many cases, this seemed to be true because households were larger, less isolated and usually included grandparents and other extended family. This meant the young mother had people all around her to assist and guide her in her parenting efforts. In many parts of America today, parents are isolated at home with a couple of young children. They may or may not know their neighbors, who may or may not have young children and who may or may not have similar family values.

Another factor is the lack of opportunities for learning parenting skills. In the smaller families of today, many older children are never around babies or have a chance to care for them. Without that experience, we have little foundation for parenting. When our first child was born, neither of us had much contact with infants, let alone full responsibility for a child. We had each done a minimum amount of babysitting as teenagers, but when we brought Nicolo home from the hospital, nothing we did felt natural. We were quickly overwhelmed by questions and anxieties, which further limited whatever nurturing instincts we had. We needed help, support and understanding, but did not know where to turn. Until that time, we had always thought that parenting would come naturally, but it doesn't.

Parenting is learned! Through the support and encouragement of other parents, by developing an understanding of our growing children, through experience, perhaps by reading and taking courses and by practicing ways of living and sharing faith, we learn how to be effective parents.

MYTH #2: THE TERRIBLE TWO'S ARE TRULY TERRIBLE

Perhaps the two most notable characteristics of the so-called "terrible two's" are the exclamation, "NO!" and frequent temper tantrums. Both are exhibited in an infinite variety of ways. For a time in his life, "no" was the only word our older son used. From the way he said it, we had to decipher whether he meant, "yes," "maybe," "I don't know," or actually, "NOOOOO!"

Our second son, on the other hand, has never really grown out of the tantrum stage. He began at about eighteen months and continues to this day. He spent ten minutes thrashing around in his room just this morning for a reason he never was very clear about. Is he stuck in the stage of, "terrible two's," or is this the dreaded, "youngest child syndrome"? When we're in the midst of his exhorting emotion, it doesn't much matter.

Our children have both exhibited the characteristics of the "terrible two's," yet we contend that most American's interpretation of this stage is a myth. Why? Because we should never let our child's developmental behavior overshadow her value as a person nor the unique bond we have with that child. This is especially true for the eighteen month to three-year-old. They are beginning to discover that they are *separate from mom or dad.* The exclamation, "NO!" is a venturing out on one's own, just for a moment, to try to discover what is ME that is not part of mom or dad.

If our posture toward this important growth step is, "These are the terrible two's ...let's gear up for battle here," then we put ourselves in an adversarial position with our child just when she needs closeness, love, understanding and a safe atmosphere to explore her new found identity the most.

Certainly the two-year-old needs limits to learn what is acceptable behavior; without them the child cannot learn to function socially. But children also need much praise and affirmation for the signals of independence and personal fortitude they show and these are the things that drive parents crazy, because a child learns early on how to push our buttons and bring us to the brink of a Mt. St. Helen's explosion.

We must continually strive to see the real person our child is, and not just the stage he is going through. When we do this, we will be able to affirm his growth and set wise limits to his aggravating behavior. Remember, this is only the first time the child will explore his personal identity; adolescence is not too far down the road. Whatever healthy patterns we develop now may last a lifetime.

TEN PARENTING SUGGESTIONS

Over the years we have been helped by ten positive parenting tips we learned from Carol V. Swingen, a clinical social worker in Portland, OR. The theme of these tips can be summed up: "I need to believe in my children, because there are times when they can't believe in themselves."

1.   Beware of doing too much for your child. Our five-year-old wants us to tie his shoes every morning because he doesn't think it is fair that he has to do it every day. On a good day, we simply remind him that his mom and dad have been tying their own shoes every day for many years. On a bad day his whining grates like fingernails on a chalk board, and one of us rushes over to tie his shoes.

Sometimes parents are the last to see their child is growing up and becoming more capable of things that once required help. Many times it's easier to just do these tasks ourselves than it is to clean up after a child's attempt, but children need to be stretched to realize their potential for accomplishment. As parents, our goal should be to activate that little voice inside that says, "I can do it. Even if I haven't done it before, I can try."

We suggest you make a list of all the things you do for your children. Which ones can you stop right away? Which ones can you let go of in a little while? Which ones will you need to hang onto?

2.   Don't label your child. Many parents have special nicknames that communicate their special love for each child. Each child is unique person, and we love them in unique ways.

But we need to be sure that those don't become labels that reinforce negative behavior ("He's our wild one!") or put pressure on a child to conform to unfair, perhaps unrealistic expectations. These labels may stick for years, even a lifetime. Rene's label as a child was the "good, perfect, quiet" child. Much of her family still looks to her to fulfill those expectations and it is hard, even as an adult, to break away from those expectations.

3.   Don't pick on your child. Leif normally handles the morning routine around our house: getting the kids up and dressed, making breakfast on the table, making sure beds are made, etc. On stressful mornings he sometimes slips into a negative communication pattern, asking the children, "How come your room is such a mess?" or, "Did you leave your coat at preschool again?" or "Can't you eat without making a mess?"

Nobody likes to be picked at, least of all a young child, and it isn't productive anyway. Things work better in the morning when roles and expectations are clearly laid out beforehand. Leif will remind them the night before: "OK boys, in the morning we're going to get dressed and make beds before breakfast, then brush our teeth and comb our hair right afterward. Then you might have some time to play before we leave." It also helps to give praise and affirmation for possible behavior. *Catch them doing things right.*

4.   Let your child answer for himself or herself. How often do you put words in your children's mouths?

> "What do you say when someone gives you something?"

> "Say 'hello' to Grandma when she says 'hello' to you."

> "Honey, the nice man asked how old you are. Can you say 'three'?"

Sometimes we act as if our children are puppets, not people. We had everything rehearsed at home; why can't our little puppet perform in public?

We know a family whose children are grown now, but all three daughters have often mentioned how their mother always talked about them as if they weren't there. Mother and daughter would visit a friend, and mother would report all the good or bad things daughter was up to all in the third person, even though daughter was sitting right there. The friend would direct a question to the daughter, and mother would chime in with the response. Then mother would berate the daughter for not being talkative with the adults!

The above example takes this habit to the extreme, but we need to allow space for our children to interact with others (especially adults) their own way. We're not saying children shouldn't be taught common social courtesy, but if we always jump in and respond for them, we don't give them a chance to practice their training. Better to affirm whatever efforts they make, however imperfect, and give them the sense that what they do say counts.

5.   Respect your child's physical privacy and rights. Leif loves to tickle our boys and hear them laugh uncontrollably with delight. Yet he realizes there is a limit that he must respect. One day after our older son had just turned five, he told us that he did not want to be tickled anymore. Leif didn't take the remark too seriously and shortly thereafter reached over and playfully tickled him. Nicolo's response was firm and serious: "Dad, if you tickle me again I'm going to call for a family meeting so we can deal with the problem." Needless to say, Leif got the message.

Every family has different standards for personal and physical privacy, and there is a wide range between fairly modest and fairly "open" that would be considered healthy. Yet the standards must be consistent for all members of the family. The best way to teach children that their bodies are their own and nobody else's, is to model that behavior at home. Little children still need help getting dressed, going to the bathroom, combing hair, etc., but a parent can perform these tasks with respect for the child. Hugs and other signs of affection should be freely given without inappropriate emotional or physical strings attached. Everyone needs to be loved and touched with respect and integrity, no matter how young they are.

6.   Plant seeds of readiness. Our younger son thinks he can do everything his older brother can do. Infamous sibling competition is perhaps the most natural way of planting seeds of readiness. Luke is convinced he can learn how to read. His older brother, who learned to read about a year ago, has discovered how useful and joyful it can be, and younger brother Luke just can't stand missing out. So we sit down with him now and then and he "reads" by telling the story as he flips the pages. We always praise and affirm his efforts and stretch him to actually recognize letters and words that appear often.

We don't believe in pushing our children ahead of their own personal growth schedule just to keep up with everyone else. But there are always those moments when the child is just around the corner from a new growth step, and a little nudge can launch them into a new stage for which they are ready. These are what the experts call "teachable moments"—those times when the child is most receptive to learning. It applies to spiritual and religious growth as well as intellectual and emotional learning.

Readiness is also an issue of esteem and confidence. As parents, if we express unfailing confidence in our children that in God's time they will learn to read, understand the Eucharist or whatever, then the child will be more receptive when the moment comes. Parent anxiety can hinder a child's growth and readiness.

7.   Give freedom from roles. Have you ever known parents who try to live out their dreams through their child? A mother who always dreamed of being a dance performer pushes and pushes her daughter in dance training; a father who almost made the big leagues drives his son to be the best ball player. What parent would not want his or her child to grow up like him or her? But we can only help our children be what God has created them to be—fully themselves.

When children are young, their gifts and personalities begin to emerge. Perhaps one shows an aptitude for music, another potential for athletic prowess. Their gifts must be encouraged, of course, but without labels like, "He's our athlete in the family, but she's the artist." Children need freedom from these roles in order to explore all their gifts. They may not have as much aptitude for other endeavors, but they should be praised and affirmed just as much for trying. What we really want are well-rounded children, so let's affirm the diversity of their gifts.

8. Show that you believe in the future. Parents can get so caught up in their day-to-day problems that the future appears either bleak or hardly worth considering. Children have an incredibly long life ahead of them, and we provide a glimpse for how it might turn out. If they see parents who are down and out, with nothing to look forward to, then they themselves will have trouble looking forward to adulthood.

Sure, there are a lot of negative things in our world today, but we must communicate a hopeful attitude. Our Catholic Christian faith demands that we see a ray of light in the darkness of life and cling to it with unyielding hope. Furthermore, our faith demands us to be moved and excited by all the events around us. The only thing worse than hopelessness is not caring at all. Our children must know that we believe in the future, otherwise they have no reason to want to grow up.

9. Show that you care about the earth. Our world is the home which God has given us. American society shows little appreciation for this gift and its limited resources. The world can ill afford another generation of resource abusers; our children must be taught to care for the earth.

If we have reverence for our world and its resources, we appreciate God's awesome creativity. And when we reflect that we are created in God's image, we grow in wonder and respect for ourselves. People who are close to the earth are close to God.

10. Keep your child bigger than whatever your problems are. We all know the feeling of being overwhelmed by the problems of our lives: mortgage payments, car repairs, plumbing problems, etc. Perhaps we've done or said something that has caused great distress and we would give anything to take it back. Whether it's an embarrassment, a financial blunder or a major mistake on the job, it always feels better to face the problem squarely and not let it envelope us.

Children's problems and mistakes are not a big deal to adults, but to them they are just as devastating. Whether the problem is tantrums or bed-wetting or making a mess at the table, a child can begin to feel overwhelmed by a problem that may seem insignificant to us. And how often do we reinforce their distress by over-reacting? Keeping the child bigger than the problem is very important because sometimes the child cannot do this for herself. One must always distinguish between the child and child's action. The child is always lovable and deserving of love, even if her actions aren't. When that happens, it is important to let her know we know she can do better and overcome the problem.

The basis of these ten suggestions is *self-esteem*. We need to believe in our children and, thus, empower them to believe in themselves. When we show respect for our children as people, they grow up with confidence and integrity. When we don't box them in with labels they grow up with fewer limitations and with a sense of adventure and endless possibilities. Finally, when we parent our children this way, they will probably parent their own children the same way.

CONCLUSION

Parenting for faith growth places an equal emphasis on parenting and faith growth; they go together. In this chapter we have tried to show that leading our children to God and leading them into adulthood are parallel, complimentary tasks. Faith development is dependent on healthy human development; while healthy emotional growth is partly dependent on healthy faith growth. We would be remiss to talk about only faith-related issues in this chapter.

What parent does not seek well-rounded growth in his or her child? What parent does not seek that bit of extra strength, courage or patience to show love for her child when she does everything possible to drive you nuts? What family does not seek some special "glue" that will hold them together in harmony even through the difficult times? For us the answer to these questions lies with the presence of God in our hearts, in our relationships with our children and in our cluttered and chaotic home.

We are certain our marriage could not last without God's guidance and healing. We know our children have been blessed with miracles when other children might have suffered greatly. These are just a few of the many ways God has acted in our lives. God has made our faith response easier because there are so many ways God has shown love, care, healing and guidance. We believe God is fully present in our lives and available to us in any moment of the day. Parenting for faith growth, to us, means helping our children grow in their own knowledge of God's presence.

4

SHARING FAITH WITH PRESCHOOL CHILDREN

This chapter is about sharing faith in our families. It's about discovering God's gracious activity in our lives at home and responding to it as a family with young children. How can we acknowledge our faith and our children's, and what can we do to enrich those experiences to recognize more fully God's presence?

It's a myth to believe we can "bring religion home;" God is already in our home, our children and ourselves! Our faith-building efforts must really center around *unveiling faith and values* at home.

In this chapter we will explore ways to share faith in the young family. What values and beliefs need to be shared? We will also discuss four challenges to parents for transmitting faith at home. First let's start with the faith of our children.

ENCOURAGING THE FAITH OF YOUNG CHILDREN

Our lives as people of faith can best be understood as a journey. In young childhood, the beginning of our faith journey, the gift of faith comes to us when we observe and imitate others, when we explore and test; it comes through feelings or sensory experiences we have at home or in church. The foundations of faith are laid when we learn to trust other people, ourselves and our world, not because we are told to but because we *experience* it that way. Our actions with our children influence their perceptions and, so, their faith much more than what we say. Our children's faith life is shaped by how we treat them and what experiences we provide for them.

Faith growth in childhood involves many central needs: approval and support, a sense of belonging and assurance, involvement in family life and exposure to a broader world. A child's faith life can be nurtured in a variety of ways which meet those needs. A key to faith growth is to develop the child's imagination and provide an order and routine which the child can trust.

Children learn and grow through their senses; through what they can see, hear, touch, taste and smell. They need to experience God as a gracious Parent and Creator of all the good gifts they have, to be encouraged to find God in the wonders around them and to realize that God is part of all life. They may not find the words to describe their idea of God, but God will speak and be revealed to them in ways they can understand. From the start, a child's life includes others outside the immediate family, and belonging to a community is very important for children (and parents) to fulfill our need to be wanted and accepted. We are trying to develop an attitude of belonging to our church family, with its rituals, symbols and stories. Children need to experience church as the place where they find friends, loving acceptance and happiness. They need to celebrate God's love and care in prayer, ritual and their own "liturgy."

We also want to speak to children about Jesus, the very special gift that God sent us. Christmas provides an especially appropriate time to introduce Jesus to the children as we relate the story of his birth. Children need us to talk about Jesus in very human terms, emphasizing his goodness and kindness. For children, Jesus' purpose for living on earth was to show us how God wants us to live and treat other people. When telling stories, we want to emphasize Jesus' caring and love for others. We try to make his life real for them by showing them they can be kind, loving, and helpful, like he was. We need to imaginatively re-tell favorite Bible stories to children in language appropriate for them, using situations they may have experienced and will understand.

Including children in family and ethnic traditions that enliven holiday and holy day seasons helps them see that God is wrapped up in family life, that families and faith are intimately connected. Our main challenge is to develop children's sense of awe and wonder and instill in them a sense of thanksgiving and community as we introduce them to God, our Creator, and to Jesus, our Lord.

SHARING FAITH

An essential aspect of our Catholic Christian faith is the belief that God is fully present in all people and everything we do. Perhaps it is hard to believe at times, but God is indeed present and active in our children. As parents and the primary educators of our children, it is up to us to create the atmosphere for them to discover God's presence and respond to it. But we can only give them what we really experience in our own lives. Consider this brief tale about the "Pearl of Great Price."

He asked me what I was looking for.

"I'm looking for the Pearl of Great Price," I said.

He slipped his hand into his pocket, drew it out, AND GAVE IT TO ME, just like that! I was dumbfounded. Then I began to protest: "Do you really want to give it to me? Don't you want to keep it for yourself? But..."

When I kept this up, he said finally, "Is it better to have the Pearl of Great Price, or to give it away?"

Now I have it, but I don't tell anyone. Some would not believe me or ridicule me. "You have the Pearl of Great Price? Hah!" Others would be jealous, or someone might steal it. Yet, I do have it. But there's that question—"Is it better to have it, or give it away?" How long will that question rob me of my joy? (Theophane, the Monk 10)

Obviously the Pearl of Great Price represents our own faith experience of Jesus. But if we do not give it away to others, our joy is robbed and the luster and richness of lived faith is lost.

It is that simple: To the extent that our faith is lived and real, we pass it on to those around us. That is why it is important to create the right atmosphere for our children to see God in us and what we do, rather than trying to push our beliefs on them blindly.

How do we create this atmosphere? Here are a few ideas.

- **Value their experience.** When we help children reflect on simple life experiences, we put them in touch with faith stories. Whether it's their first encounter with ocean waves, a conflict over sharing toys or learning to tell the truth, we reinforce our belief that God is active in their lives.

- **Introduce the wisdom of the community.** Keeping in mind the child's simple life experiences, we share a piece of the Catholic faith story (incarnation, death and resurrection of Jesus) that pertains to his or her small faith story.

■ **Create an atmosphere of dialogue.** Here we attempt to relate their story with the story of our faith. We want them to see that the God of our faith, who has been at work throughout history, is at work in their lives and in their story.

■ **Gently challenge toward response.** We ask a few questions and make a few suggestions to help our children live their faith. We cannot force a response but try to encourage and support their living response to God.

We believe family life creates a conducive atmosphere for sharing faith and values. As we learn more about the powerful influences of our family of origin, we see that tremendous emotional energy, attitudes and personality characteristics are transmitted from one generation to the next, along with faith and values.

Unfortunately, many obstacles can block moments of faith growth or prevent the family from capitalizing on faith opportunities. For instance, many parents demand the religious formation of their children but do not continue to grow in their own faith. This sends a mixed message to children who wonder why the Catholic faith should be important for them but not for their parents. Another obstacle can be the values and influences we receive from our society which run counter to the teachings of Jesus and the Church. These influences are a real challenge to religious faith in our lives and our children's lives. A third obstacle is often our inability to see God's activity in the clutter and chaos of our daily lives.

In spite of these obstacles the powerful influences of the family prevail, and through our family experience we gain our sense of Catholic Christian identity. The presence of God is contagious, and given the right atmosphere, we will pass it on to those around us. Therefore our greater challenge lies not only in providing quality religious experiences for our children but also for ourselves.

SHARING THE CATHOLIC FAITH STORY

What teachings of Jesus and Church are we supposed to share with our children? We believe our Catholic Christian heritage is richer and more personal than a simple list of beliefs, prayers, doctrines and rules. So we ask ourselves, what are the basic themes that encompass this richness of our faith? We look for the simple but strong statements that truly name truths, traditions and daily experiences of what it means to be a Catholic Christian. If we can name these strong, simple truths for ourselves, we will have the foundation to share living faith with our children.

"What do Christians need to know in order to become disciples?" It is important to distinguish between understanding faith and having a faith understanding. We can understand the Christian faith intellectually, but to pass on the richness of our Christian heritage requires a certain element of personal religious experience, grounded in faith but occurring as part of one's awareness of life. Faith understanding involves a recognition of God's activity in our lives, and sharing our knowing of God with those around us. This is no small task.

And yet there is more. We must share *accurate understandings* of faith, not just our wonderful feelings of God. There is always a danger of making God into our image and likeness rather than vice versa. People need relatively few basic religious understandings; but these must be true. Let's look at five fundamental understandings that we can share with our children.

The Church

Beyond the church of the home, the parish community is the most important expression of church. There is nothing more powerful and successful at communicating messages of Christian faith than a community of believers. Learning, worshipping and serving with other like-minded people allows us all to grasp the meaning and challenge of Jesus' life, death and resurrection which is our salvation.

Remember though, the church is a group of people gathered together in faith, not the building on the corner or its bureaucracy. Our children need to see (and understand) that when families gather in faith, whether at home, in church, at the cemetery or on the front steps of the local courthouse, that is "church" in the spiritual sense.

Just as important, our children (and perhaps many parents) must learn that you don't have to go to church to reach God. Rather, each one of us as believers can bring God's presence to others. God is in our midst, and the church (gathering of believers) is where we encounter God.

Jesus Christ

The life, death and resurrection of Jesus provides the foundation of our Catholic Christian faith. Our belief in Jesus is what distinguishes us from other religious believers. It is therefore paramount to teach a correct understanding of Jesus to our children.

How often do we hear expressions like "Do the Christian thing" or "Do you have a Christian attitude toward others?" Although these expressions are used to try to convince people to think and do good things, if they are heard too often the definition of what it means to be Christian becomes removed from Jesus, the Christ. Our children need to understand and know Jesus.

Who is Jesus, really? What should we say about him? Jesus came from Nazareth in Galilee. He preached the nearness of the Kingdom of God and connected its coming with his own words and deeds. He called people to conversion, to hear God's words of love and challenge them to become disciples. He was a teacher and a prophet who used stories and images to communicate his vision of world in which there would be harmony, justice, peace, human togetherness, equality, love and forgiveness. He gathered people who were considered outcasts and sinners together and ate and drank with them, offering them God's unconditional love and healing their illnesses. He had a very special relationship with God, calling God Abba (Father). He was a man of prayer. He believed in the equality of all people, calling women and men alike to follow him. His message and actions brought him into conflict with the Jewish and Roman authorities. Eventually he was crucified by the Roman authorities.

But the story does not end there. We believe that on the third day, God raised Jesus from the dead. We believe that the risen Lord Jesus lived in the first disciples as they continued his mission. We believe that the risen Lord Jesus continues to live in his disciples and church today. Here lies the challenge of faith in our attempts to grasp and communicate the reality of the risen Jesus. Very simply, we believe that Jesus is alive and offers a relationship to those who believe. Implied in this relationship is a call to worship with other believers and to serve those who Jesus himself would serve.

Faith in God

As believers in Jesus we are led to the mystery of God. What should we teach our children about God? We should tell them what Jesus taught about God. The very purpose of Jesus' life, death and resurrection was to lead others to God. Everything Jesus said and did reveals who God is. The Good News found in the Gospels reveals to us the God of Jesus.

We know that God cares for us and loves us. God invites us into a living relationship, a relationship of faith. This relationship is a gift from God. Our response to God's gift is Christian living. We are called to develop a loyal and trusting relationship with God and with God's people. We are called to love God, self and others. We are called to discover God through our family relationships. We are called to draw upon the wisdom of the Bible and the Catholic Christian Tradition to give meaning to our lives. We are called to live our faith in the world based on the vision and values of Jesus and the Church. We are called to live and work for justice, peace and human dignity.

In teaching our children about God and faith in God, it is important to emphasize that faith is a free gift, that it is a relationship initiated by God, and that God very much desires our response. It is also important to emphasize that our response is lived out in our relationships, our beliefs, and our actions.

Prayer—Communication with God

How can we communicate with God? Prayer is our faith response to God's revelation. God always takes the initiative. Contrary to the common belief that prayer is our turning to God for what we need, and then God answers, we believe that God speaks first and our response is prayer. God is always present and active in our lives, and our prayers are a response to this gracious presence. The more aware we are of how, where and when God speaks, the more "fruitful" our communication with God will be.

In teaching our children to pray, we should focus as much on how they "hear" God speaking to them as on their speaking to God. Encourage your child to sense God's presence all around them in her daily life. God can also be found deep inside our feelings. Occasionally, children will literally burst forth with communication to God as they become more and more aware of how fully present God is. A good example of this is prayers of thanksgiving.

Because children often have relationships with someone or something that, to them, is real but unseen, prayer can be easier for them than adults. They have tremendous imagination which they can use to know God better. They will often develop images of God, made up or borrowed from adults, and with our help they can find images of God in Scripture, the Catholic Tradition and our own experience that will help them grow.

The Bible is a key teaching tool to help children develop their relationship and communication with God. Our Scriptures tell the stories of who God is in history. In using the Bible with our children, we must be careful to relate what it actually says and means rather than justify what we would like to say. This does not mean we must all be scripture scholars, but we must respect the Word of God for what it is.

Finally, our prayers must not be self-centered or self-serving. God takes the initiative. We respond with prayers of joy, thanksgiving, petition. We can be sure God's Spirit works for the good of all, wherever people are concerned for others, and this must be the focus of our communication with God.

Christian Living

What does it mean to live as a Christian today? To live as a Christian requires an understanding of sin, reconciliation and discipleship.

Our children must know that sin is real and that all people are capable of turning away from God's gracious love. Without placing any unrealistic expectations on children or loading them with unreasonable burdens of guilt, they can grasp, at a very young age, that Christian living calls for Christian behavior.

When they fall short of expectations, they can say, "I'm sorry," and expect the same response when people have wronged them. Reconciliation is being aware of and responding to the invitation to accept God's love again. God is always offering us healing and reconciliation. Children need to know that God is not "angry" with them, but that God is a gracious parent, always loving them.

Christian living involves more than just avoiding sin. Christian living is hearing God's call to *discipleship*. For young children, discipleship primarily means living freely as a child and remaining open to the great love and acceptance God shows them.

FOUR CHALLENGES FOR PARENTS

Raising our children in a faith-filled Christian atmosphere is perhaps our most important parenting task. To live out this vocation we must respond to four specific challenges. These fulfill our own Christian call as parents with a special responsibility for sharing faith with the next generation. These four challenges reflect the realities of today's society.

1.   Be a belonger as well as a believer.

In 1989 a Gallup Poll found that the vast majority of Americans claim to be "believers." They believe in God, pray, sense God's presence in the world, "see" God in nature, etc. Yet they also found that a great many Americans do not claim to be "belongers." Many say they do not need a church or community of believers to know God. They have a purely vertical relationship with God, or at best, find God's presence in a stunning sunset, in waves crashing on a beach or in the cute things their children do.

Christian parents are challenged to be belongers as well as believers. We can still discover God in beautiful spring flowers but our faith is based on the life, ministry, death and resurrection of Jesus Christ. To grasp the full meaning of our salvation requires the wisdom and lived experience of a community of believers, both in the present and throughout history. We have a rich, deep faith heritage that renders God's presence in the sunset or waves all the more meaningful.

Christianity has always been a communal faith. Remember that Jesus gathered a community of disciples when he was alive and entrusted his mission to a community of disciples when he rose. This community of disciples, the Church, continues to communicate and live Jesus' vision and values. Viewing Christianity as a communal faith is especially difficult in a highly individualistic society like ours. We need the support and challenge of a community to live our Catholic faith today. Our children need a community of faith from which they can learn about Jesus Christ and how to live as Catholic Christians today. We all need a community of faith to celebrate our relationship with God through Sunday worship and the celebration of the sacraments. To really know God, we must be belongers as well as believers.

2.   Be a role model for your children.

Everyone has heard the phrase, "You can't give what you ain't got." If we want our children to grow in faith and live as Catholic Christians, our own faith must be real and alive. Otherwise, we cannot pass it on. Too many parents expect their parish, alone, to make disciples of their children. This isn't fair to the parish or healthy for your children. In the end it will not be enough.

Let's say, for example, that your child is preparing for first Eucharist and has a question about Sunday Mass. You can't remember the answer you learned when you were a child, so you feel embarrassed and inadequate. But the answer from your childhood is not what your child needs to hear. What is more helpful is for you to share what Eucharist means to you now. What is your experience of Eucharist each Sunday morning? What roles does it play in your life? Why is it important? Answering these questions is a faith challenge for all of us. You can share your childhood memories, not about what you were taught, but about how important it was for you to receive Communion. Sharing your stories are meaningful ways to share faith.

3. Give priority to faith formation.

In our neighborhood there is great social pressure to enroll our children in everything from gymnastics to soccer to woodworking classes. While it is healthy for children to receive proper athletic and social formation, as Christian parents we are also challenged to try to give equal time to their faith formation.

Athletics and other organized activities can teach children a lot, but some families seem to lose perspective. Can you imagine if all parents were as dedicated to the faith enrichment of their children as many are to their children's soccer team? If we practice soccer or baseball with our children, we should also work with them on their First Eucharist preparation; if we coach their sports team this year, maybe we should be a catechist next year. If we show that personal faith enrichment is as important as our own recreation, that message will be more easily communicated to our children.

4. Celebrate rituals at home.

Catholic Christianity is rich in symbols, signs and rituals. We are a sacramental church. We employ concrete signs to help us embrace the real but unseen God. We believe not only in the seven major sacraments but that any moment of our lives is "sacramentalized" with God's presence. Our symbols and rituals are extremely valuable. Yet we live in a society that does not often value these things. Attending Mass once a week just does not provide the full richness of ritual and symbol that our faith expression provides us. All families need to explore rituals and rites of passage at home.

Many families incorporate daily, weekly or seasonal rituals. One family may tell a story about Jesus and friends at the dinner table while another may give their children a simple blessing on the forehead when tucking them into bed. Some families make a "ritual" of performing community service regularly or perhaps going out for brunch after Sunday Mass. Thanksgiving, Christmas and Easter offer opportunities for family rituals. When we include these activities at home, our parish worship is all the more meaningful.

One of our family rituals involves Ash Wednesday, when each of us draws a symbol of personal weakness that we intend to work on during Lent. This may range from vowing to make my bed each day, to putting on a happy face, to helping someone. We have a simple meal on Wednesday night and share our symbols, then put our drawings in a foil-covered dish and burn them as our offering to the Lord. Then we put the ashes in a small jar on the dinner table where everyone can see them. Throughout Lent, we say to each other, "Remember your ashes," which serves as a gentle reminder of our promises.

We also celebrate significant rites of passage in our family. Some changes mean greater independence and responsibility for a family member, others mean new surroundings for the entire family. When we moved, we experienced many changes, including new neighbors, a new school and a new parish. To ritualize this, we invited friends (some old and some new) for a simple blessing for our new home.

We also celebrate such rites of passage as birthdays, anniversaries, new jobs, a child learning how to walk or a teenager getting a driver's license. We know of one family who had an impromptu blessing of their youngsters' bikes on the day the youngest finally learned how to ride, celebrating the wonderful freedom and independence of "having wheels."

Exploring ritual and rites of passage helps families recognize that God is a part of our daily lives, and that we have access to God through the richness of symbol and ritual.

Works Cited

Theophane, the Monk. *Tales of a Magic Monastery*. New York: Crossroad Publishing, 1981.

5

STRATEGIES AND ACTVITIES

SHARING THE CATHOLIC FAITH STORY

Families play a key role in sharing the values and beliefs of the Catholic community. This is done when:

- all family members, especially adults, continue to grow in their own faith through reading, informal discussion or participation in parish or community educational programs and share their learnings with one another;

- families participate in intergenerational catechetical experiences, gathering with other families to learn, grow, and live the Catholic faith;

- families make the connection between their life experiences and faith values, drawing on the rich resources of Scripture, Catholic Tradition and the faith traditions found in their ethnic heritage;

- families participate together in the sacramental preparation of individual family members;

- families recognize the impact of media and learn to evaluate media critically in light of the life-giving values of the Catholic Christian faith.

The following activities provide examples of how the Catholic faith story can be shared meaningfully by families with children of preschool age.

1. TALKING TOGETHER ABOUT GOD

When do children start learning about God? Probably at the moment of birth. Learning about others is about a lot more than words. It is about thoughts and feelings, relationships and experiences. Children learn about God from the things and the people that surround them. From the wonder they experience in life. From the love they experience from family and friends. Talking with young children about God helps them to locate God within the framework of the experiences that make up their life. Simple God-talk that would make sense to young children includes:

God as creator: creating for us, giving us to use all the beautiful things that surround us—pets and wild animals, house plants and giant trees, sunshine and showers, and especially people.

God as loving parent: caring about them and about all people, wanting everyone to have what they need to grow.

Jesus, God's special Son: reminding us of how much God loves us, caring about people, telling us how God wants us to live.

God-talk with young children will make sense only insofar as it echoes their experience of life. A good rule of thumb is: If you can't find a parallel between the faith value you'd like to share and the experience of the child, it's probably too early to share it! Talk of the miracles of Jesus or events in his life like the transfiguration or resurrection are beyond the comprehension of little ones and should be set aside until later in life.

Talking with toddlers and preschoolers is most easily done informally, using their life experiences as teachable moments to talk about God. Common experiences like a hug and kiss before bedtime provide an opportunity to let children know that God loves them equally as much as you do. An autumn walk through falling leaves or night time peek at the moon and stars can reinforce the image of God as creator. Family celebrations of Christmas and Easter can reveal a lot to children about how important God is to your family and teach simple lessons about Jesus' humanity and concern for others.

Helping children feel "at home" with God during their first few years of life provides a firm foundation for later sharing of Christian values.

Learn More About It:

Leslie, Karen. *Faith and Little Children: A Guide for Parents and Teachers*. Mystic, CT: Twenty-Third Publications, 1990.

2. SHARING FAITH THROUGH VIDEOS

Video can be a wonderful means of sharing faith values with young children. The following sampler contains just a few of the many resources being created today for families with young children. Contact your parish or diocesan media library or the distributor listed for further information on the videos or to see about borrowing, renting or purchasing the materials listed. Unless otherwise indicated the the videos are available through Don Bosco Multimedia, P.O. Box T, New Rochelle, NY 10802-0845 (800-342-5850)

The Amazing Book. A fully animated captivating way to teach children about the Bible. *The Amazing Book* will appeal to children ages two through ten and give them a love for the Book of books that will last forever. [28 minutes] Distributed by: Credence Cassettes, P.O. Box 419491, Kansas City, MO 64141-6491 (800-333-7373)

Bible Stories from Hanna-Barbera. Eleven wonderful Bible stories told by the world's best known cartoon maker. Exciting, believable, joyous! [30 minutes each—11 videos]

The Human Race Club. Character building through stories, ideal for pre-school and kindergarten children. [22-28 minutes each—6 videos]
Titles: *Self Esteem, "The Letter on Light Blue Stationery"; Earning Money, "A High Price to Pay"; Making Friends, "The Fair Weather Friend"; Fights Between Brothers and Sisters "Casey's Revenge"; Handling Emotions, "The Lean Mean Machine"; Prejudice and Discrimination, "The Unforgettable Pen Pal"*

McGee and Me! Young and old alike will delight in the adventures and scrapes encountered by eleven-year-old Nicholas and his animated buddy, McGee. Packed full of biblical values, *McGee and Me!* was created to be both entertaining and spiritually enlightening. [30 minutes each— 9 videos]
Titles: *Take Me Out of the Ball Game, 'Twas the Fight Before Christmas, The Big Lie, A Star in the Breaking, The Not-So-Great Escape, Skate Expectations, Twister and Shout, Back to the Drawing Board, Do the Bright Thing*

Music Machine. Over a million copies of the *Music Machine* book and cassette have enchanted listeners from age two to adults. Now, through the magic of full animation, you can visit the colorful kingdom of Agapeland where a wonderful

blend of stories and songs gently teach about the fruit of the spirit. [28 minutes]
Distributed by: Credence Cassettes, P.O. Box 419491, Kansas City, MO 64141-6491 (800-333-7373)

Our Friends on Wooster Square. Here is an exciting, fun-filled faith sharing program for young Christians. Based on the same educational research used by Children's Television Workshop (Sesame Street), the staff at Pastoral Theological Institute has created *Our Friends on Wooster Square.* Each program explores through storyline, song and Scripture a single word or concept. Here is a tested, fun-filled, entertaining and exciting program for children five to eight years old. [60 minutes each—Series I and II, 30 minutes each—Series III]
Distributed by: Franciscan Communications, 1229 South Santee St., Los Angeles, CA 90015-2566 (800-421-8510)

Learn More About It:

Roberto, John ed. *Media, Faith, and Families: A Parents' Guide to Family Viewing.* New Rochelle, NY: Don Bosco Multimedia, 1992.

3. READ A CHILD A STORY OF FAITH

Young children love to be read to from picture books. In fact, they often love to be read to from the same two or three books over, and over, and over again. Introduce them to books and stories that speak simply of faith and Christian values. Some of these books may be intentionally "Christian." Others may highlight Christian values without the word "Christian" ever appearing in print. In either case, find a good story, and share it with a young child.

Augsburg Publishing House (Minneapolis, MN) publishes a wonderful series of *Dear God* books. Written and illustrated by Annie Fitzgerald, the books celebrate children's questions about and wonder in God. Among the titles in the *Dear God* series are the following: *Dear God, Let's Play!*; *Dear God, Thanks for Making Me...Me!*; *Dear God, I Just Love Birthdays*; and *Dear God, Where Do You Live?*

A great resource for identifying good reading material for children of all ages is *The New York Times Parents' Guide to the Best Books for Children* edited by Eden Ross Lipson. The Guide provides brief descriptions of hundreds of readily available books suitable for reading with young children.

If you get tired of reading preschoolers the same story over and over again, consider reading it one final time and taping your performance for later use by your child. Or check out the array of tape-books available on the market.

Learn More About It:

Hearne, Betsy. *Choosing Books for Children: A Commonsense Guide.* New York: Delacorte Press, 1990.

Lipson, Eden Ross, ed. *The New York Times Parents' Guide to the Best Books for Children.* New York: Times Books, 1991.

Trelease, Jim. *The New Read Aloud Handbook.* New York: Penguin, 1989.

Winkel, Lois and Sue Kimmel. *Mother Goose Comes First: An Annotated Buide to the Best Books and Recordings for your Preschool Child.* New York: Holt, 1990.

4. CHURCH BUILDING TOUR

Little children find church buildings fascinating. Their size and shape, decorations and furnishings make them unlike any of the other "houses" they regularly find themselves in. Touring the church building in your parish can be a good way of helping your child feel more at home in the parish and sharing some basic facts about the Catholic faith story.

Keep your explanations and descriptions simple. Connect your explanations, insofar as possible, with experiences your child is already familiar with. Use the following approach on your tour or create one of your own.

Before the visit or on the way.

Children know that families sometimes come together on special occasions to talk and eat, pray and sing. Describe the building you will be visiting as the place where the church family does the same things! Because the church family is large, the building needs to be large, too. You and your child are part of the church family. Like the buildings on your street or in your neighborhood, church buildings don't all look exactly alike. But if you look closely there are usually hints like a cross or bell or special, stained glass window that tell us the building we're looking at is a church.

Inside the building.

Even young children understand that people act special in special places. Explain that the church building is one of those places. It's a place for walking not running, and a place where people usually talk quietly. That way, when it's filled with people, everyone can hear and pay attention.

Try to experience the sights, sounds, smells and textures of the church building through your child's senses. Being alone in the building, without lots of big people blocking your child's view or distracting his/her attention from the building, will make the experience a new one. Some of the things your child will see will prompt the need for a simple explanation.

The statues and figures seen in the stained glass windows are images of some special friends of God and of the church family. Point out figures that your child may know, especially images of Mary and Joseph and any saints who carry the same names as your family members.

The altar is the church family's table. The church family comes together every day to share a special meal of bread and wine around the table. Candles are lit during the meal, just like they are at special meals at home.

Similar simple explanations should suffice for a young child. Return regularly or visit other church buildings in your area. More important than the explanations is the comfort your child should feel with the building tour and with knowing he is part of the church family.

CELEBRATING RITUALS AND PRAYING TOGETHER

Families provide a sense of rhythm and celebration to their faith life by celebrating unique family rituals and participating in the ritual life of the parish community. This is done when:

- families celebrate the many ways that the sacred is revealed in their shared life through home rituals focused on ordinary family events, important milestones in family life, liturgical seasons and appropriate civic holidays;

- families regularly participate in the Sunday Eucharistic assembly;

- families actively participate in parish rituals that support and complement their home rituals and celebrations;

- all family members actively participate in the preparation and celebration of the sacramental rites of passage of family members through in-home activities and participation in parish programs;

- families reclaim, affirm and celebrate their own ethnic rituals and traditions, and participate in cultural and ethnic celebrations offered by the parish community and the wider Church and civic community.

Families encourage the development of a family prayer life and involve family members in the prayer life of the parish community. This is done when:

- parents and adult family members continue to grow by devoting time and care to their relationship with God through spiritual development programs and resources;

- families develop a pattern of family prayer which nurtures faith and sustains the family during times of change or crisis;

- parents help their children to pray in age-appropriate ways;

- families join with others in the parish community for prayer and support;

- families draw upon their ethnic prayer traditions in creating their family prayer pattern and draw on the cultural and ethnic prayer traditions of the extended family, parish, and wider church community;

- parents encourage participation of family members in age-specific spiritual development programs and prayer experiences/services and connect an individual's experience in these programs to the family's prayer life.

The following activities provide practical examples of how families with preschool children can share together in ritual and prayer.

1. A FAMILY ADVENT CALENDAR

A family Advent calendar helps people keep track of the days leading up to Christmas. It serves as a daily reminder that the birth of Jesus is the reason behind the season and helps family members pause for a few minutes each day to think about the importance of Jesus in their life and in the life of the world.

Advent calendars can be purchased in most card shops and religious bookstores. An even better approach, however, is to involve the whole family in making an Advent calendar of your own.

Using poster board and construction paper, magazine photos and whatever else strikes your fancy, create a picture of a family home, a neighborhood scene or a Christmas creche. Behind the doors, shutters and other possible hiding places in your picture (under a nest in the tree or rock in yard) draw or paste pictures or symbols that carry a special Advent message for your family. Tape construction paper shutters over the windows and doors so they can be opened easily to reveal your message. Make sure there is a message (and hiding place) for each of the days between the first Sunday of Advent and Christmas day. Put a number over each hiding place, starting at the highest number, and working down gradually to your Christmas message.

Each message should help your family in their preparation for Christmas. Be creative in deciding what messages you will use in your Advent calendar. If possible, divide up the messages among family members so that ever day's message is a surprise for someone in the family. Messages can include:

- Simple scripture passages, e.g., 1 John 3:11 (This is the message taught from the beginning: We must love one another) or Matthew 5:14, 16 (Your are the light of the world; your light must shine before others so they see the good things you do and praise your God in heaven).

- A family-enriching, Christmas preparation activity, like making dough ornaments together for the Christmas tree, deciding on a special gift you can buy as a family for a child from a poor family or reading together a children's picture book on the birth of Jesus.

- A faith question to discuss together, e.g., why is Christmas so special or what does Santa have to do with Jesus?

- A family, fun-time suggestion, e.g., sing the Fa La La song together, call grandma and tell her how much you love her, hug each other two or three times.

Put your Advent calendar in a prominent place in your home. Choose a regular time during the day when you can all be together to uncover your message. Light a candle and say a simple prayer before your "grand opening."

A simple prayer like the following is appropriate for families with young children:

Thank you, Jesus, for loving us.

As we get ready to celebrate your birth on Christmas day, help us to share our love even more with each other. Amen!

Learn More About It:

Halmo, Joan. *Celebrating the Church Year with Young Children.* Collegeville, MN: The Liturgical Press, 1988.
Roberto, John, ed. *Family Rituals and Celebrations.* New Rochelle, NY: Don Bosco Multimedia, 1992.

2. A CHRISTMAS CRECHE

A Christmas creche is a wonderful visual for children. They can use it to see, touch and talk about the key characters in the Christmas story. Your family creche can be made together or selected together from the variety of creche sets available for purchase in religious goods stores, Christmas shops and department stores. Many religious goods stores and museum shops now offer creche sets from different parts of the world featuring, for example, clay figures from Mexico, brightly painted wooden characters from El Salvador and sturdy plastic, classical reproductions from Italy and France. Pick a set that fits your tastes and that is large and tough enough to be regularly handled by young children.

Set aside some special time as a family, during Advent or on Christmas eve, to set up your creche. Use the following process or create one of our own:

- Read the story of Jesus' birth in Bethlehem from a children's Bible or a good children's picture book.

- Discuss the story together, trying to breathe life for young children into the characters and events. Ask simple questions like: What do you think the city was like that Mary and Joseph were traveling to? How did they feel as they walked around looking for a place to stay? How did they feel when they finally found one? Where do you think the shepherds thought the music was coming from? How did they feel when the angel appeared? How would you feel if an angel suddenly appeared here! Why are we happy that Jesus was born that night?

- Choose and arrange the spot where your creche set will be displayed for the Christmas season.

- Take the creche figures out one at a time, identifying them and the role they play in the Christmas story. Allow children to carefully hold and touch the figures. Decide together where each figure should be placed.

- When all the figures are in place, light a candle and have one of the family members read the following prayer:

> Lord, bless this creche. Help us always to be like the Christ child who is in love with his God.
>
> May the presence of the creche in our home remind us of how much God loves us.
>
> May we grow, every day, in love for one another, for our family, for our friends and for all the people of the world.

- Close by sharing kisses and hugs with family members and singing together a Christmas carol like *Silent Night* or *Angels We Have Heard on High*.

3. EASTER EGGS

Which came first, the rabbit or the egg? Probably the egg! Eggs are an ancient symbol of fertility and new life. They seem empty and lifeless until new life suddenly bursts from the shell. Hundreds of years ago the simple egg was adopted by Christians as a powerful symbol of faith.

Jesus, who is the source of new life for Christians, burst forth from the seemingly lifeless tomb on Easter morning. As a way of proclaiming their belief in Jesus' resurrection, Christians began the practice of giving one another eggs on Easter Sunday.

To convey the joy and beauty of Easter, they carefully painted and decorated the eggs they shared. In fact, in some ethnic cultures decorating eggs has become a prized art form, passed on from generation to generation. Decorating eggs on

Holy Saturday is a wonderful Easter tradition in which even young children can take part.

Before the egg-decorating process begins:

- Read the gospel account of Jesus' resurrection from your family children's Bible.

- Explain the beliefs that underlie the practice of egg decorating: Jesus rose from the dead; Jesus is new life for us and for our world.

- Note that the bright colors and designs on the egg show our joy in Jesus' resurrection.

After the eggs have been decorated, bless them for use by your family and friends:

- Place the eggs in a decorative basket or bowl;

- Put them on the table with a lighted candle and a Bible opened to the account of Jesus' resurrection;

- Hold hands around the table as one of your family members reads the following prayer:

> Loving God, we rejoice in Jesus' resurrection from the dead.
> We thank you for the new ways of living and loving that Jesus showed us.
> May these brightly colored Easter eggs bring joy to the people we share them with and remind them of how much Jesus cares about them.
> Alleluia, Amen!

4. EVERYDAY PRAYERS AND BLESSINGS

Blessing Before Meals

We thank you God for all the blessings you share with us.

We thank you especially for Jesus, our brother and his wonderful story about your great love for us.

We thank you for the gifts of family and friends and food.

May the blessings of your peace and love be at our table today.

Amen.

Thanksgiving After Meals

We thank you, our God,
for the food you have shared with us.

May we be strengthened by these gifts to continue your work in our world.

We ask this through Christ our Lord. Amen.

A Simple Blessing for Daily Departures

Mark the usual daily departures for work or shopping, day care or nursery school with simple blessings like the following:

> Remember God's love! May God be with you in everything you do today.

or

> May God bless your day with new experiences and new ideas, new friends and a new joy in life.

Bedtime Blessings: A Parent's Prayer for a Child

Lord, bless this child.

As you have filled his/her day with sights and sounds, activities and relationships, bless his/her night with restful sleep and pleasant dreams.

May he/she be strengthened by tonight's sleep for the new life and growth that tomorrow are sure to bring.

We ask this in Jesus' name. Amen.

Learn More About It:

Catholic Household Prayers and Blessings. Washington, DC: United States Catholic Conference.

5. CELEBRATION FOR A BIRTHDAY

Birthdays are a special time for people of almost any age. Adding a brief birthday prayer to the day's celebration helps us recall how much God loves us and how big a part of our family life God is. The prayer can be used before or after a special family birthday meal or be incorporated into a birthday celebration with family and friends.

Prayer for the Birthday Child

> God, we give you special thanks today for creating the life of (name). We thank you for all the ways we are blessed through his/her presence in our family. We ask that (name) continue to grow in age, in learning and in sharing his/her many talents and gifts with others. We are very happy that he/she is part of our family! We give you thanks in Jesus' name. Amen.

As the prayer is being read, family members can extend their hands in blessing toward the birthday child. The blessing closes with a congratulatory kisses and hugs.

Learn More About It:

Kelley, Gail. *Traditionally Yours: Telling the Christian Story through Family Traditions.* San Jose: Resource Publications, Inc., 1987.

ENRICHING FAMILY RELATIONSHIPS

Families encourage the individual growth of family members and the development of meaningful relationships within and beyond the family. This is done when:

- parents grow in their understanding of the parenting skills needed at each stage of the family life cycle;
- families work to improve their communications, decision-making and problem-solving skills;

- families work at and enjoy spending quality time together;

- families participate in intergenerational family activities which build community among family members and between families in the parish community;

- married couples consciously work at enriching their marriage relationship;

- single, divorced, separated or widowed adults work at enriching their lives and relationships through programs, support groups and resources that address their specific needs;

- families seek support and counseling during times of loss, sudden change, unexpected crises, problems and family or personal transitions.

The following activities provide practical examples of how family relationships can be nurtured and enriched during the preschool years.

1. FACTORS IN QUALITY PARENTING

The following factors have been identified as essential for quality parenting. As you read through the list, identify the things you are already doing well as a parent. Choose one or two areas that you can choose to make your parenting even more effective.

Parents spend time alone with each child. Even only children may not have a parent's undivided attention often during the week. Everything that needs to be done *for* a child may get done. But it takes a different kind of attention to do things *with* a child. The need for one-on-one time with parents can be particularly strong in families with several children and in blended families where children need the security of a special relationship with their natural parent. Quality time spent with individual children lessens competition for parental attention and can build greater cooperation among family members.

The child is the center of attention. Focusing occasional undivided attention on the events and activities that are part of a child's life builds a child's self-worth and lets him/her know how valued she is by the family. Giving special attention to "small" events in a child's life can make them "big" events in the family's history.

The whole family does it together. Doing things together as a family builds a sense of belonging and security in children. Shared experiences, traditions and rituals mark a family's life as unique and provide a strong sense of identity. Enjoyable experiences shared together create a reservoir of cooperation and good will on which families can draw in times of change and turmoil.

Kids can count on it. Experiences and activities repeated on a regular basis provide children with a sense of order. Repetition is important, especially for young children. It can be a "security blanket" that keeps life manageable for them even in the midst of change. Sharing experiences or working together on common tasks can strengthen the ties among family members and let children know that they are an important and needed part of the family.

Parents put kids' needs first. Even young children are aware of how busy life can be for parents and how many things need to get done during the day to keep family life moving ahead. Therefore, they appreciate the times when a parent sets aside her own preferences or needs and puts the child's preferences or needs first. Parents also need to be aware of and respond to their own needs. Seeing a parent's willingness to set her own needs aside for others can create a willingness on the child's part to occasionally do the same.

Parents show they care. Parents express their care in many ways: when they comfort a sick child, show empathy for a child's problems or concern, assist children with work they have to do or help children create a daily routine so they can manage their time responsibly. Caring can also be shown through shared activities and attentive conversation.

Kids feel grown up. Asking children's opinions and respecting their preferences offer them opportunities to think and act grown up. Listening to their concerns, involving them (even in a limited way) in family decisions and explaining why certain choices are made do the same. While no parent wants her child to grow up too quickly, providing children with reasonable choices gives them the confidence and self-esteem needed to meet the new challenges that growth inevitably brings.

Everyone is relaxed. Quality parenting cannot thrive in a situation filled with tension. While tension is a normal part of contemporary life, family members *can* choose to work at making home life as comfortable and relaxed as possible. Nurture humor in the family. Work at being more relaxed and effective as parents without expecting your family will ever be totally easy-going or perfect. Sometimes even relaxation takes hard work.

Parents make it fun. Sharing enjoyable activities together strengthens family relationships and communications. Parents can promote fun in the family by doing the unexpected, that is, putting a new twist in the usual routine, turning dull tasks into family games or injecting humor whenever and wherever possible.

Learn More About It:

Albert, Linda and Michael Popkin. *Quality Parenting.* New York: Ballantine Books, 1987.

2. SPECIAL CHILD NIGHT

As children grow they develop a social calendar all their own. Trying to keep family calendars balanced and guarantee quality time for family relationships can be a difficult task. Whether you are a family with one, young child or a multiple-child family that spans many years, know that every child appreciates special recognition and quality time with his/her parents. Many families have adopted a tradition called Special Child Nights as a way of building special parent-child time into their crowded family schedules. On Special Child Night, scheduled weekly or biweekly, an individual child in the family gets an hour or two of special, after-supper time with his/her parent(s). What's done during the evening is planned by the child. It could be quiet time spent reading together, work on a puzzle or craft project, laughing and talking together or anything else the child values doing with his/her parent(s).

The constant in this mix of activities is the parent's undivided attention. Household tasks, phone calls and responses to the needs of others in the family are put on hold for the duration of Special Child time. As children grow in appreciation of their own Special Night, they learn to respect other's special time and keep unnecessary interruptions to a minimum.

Some families begin Special Night with dinner, providing a seat of honor and special place setting for the chosen child. Other families start Special Night at 7:00, after the dishes have been done and any foreseeable disruptions eliminated. More important than the activities planned or the length of time set aside is the specialness of the relationship that develops between parent and child. When instituted and honored on a regular basis, Special Child's Night creates open lines of communication and builds a sense of acceptance and specialness among all participants. If you'd like to institute Special Child's Night in your home:

- Set a time frame for your evening.

- Reserve the night in advance, marking it on family, school and work calendars.

- Let everyone in the family know what's expected of them on Special Child Night.

- Once a regular schedule has been established, try not to stray from your prearranged dates.

- Within reason, stick with your child's wishes on how your time together should be spent.

- Make snack and prayer a part of your time together.

Learn More About It:

Albert, Linda and Michael Popkin. *Quality Parenting.* New York: Ballantine Books, 1987.

Dinkmeyer Sr., Don et al. *Parenting Young Children.* Circle Pines, MN: American Guidance Services, 1989.

Kelley, Gail. *Traditionally Yours: Telling the Christian Story Through Family Traditions.* San Jose, CA: Resource Publications, Inc., 1987.

Sullivan, S. Adams. *The Quality Time Almanac: A Sourcebook of Ideas and Activities for Parents and Kids.* Garden City, NY: Doubleday and Company, 1986.

3. JUST FOR YOU: ENRICHING YOUR ADULT RELATIONSHIPS

Caring for children takes a lot of time and energy. As you work to build a respectful encouraging relationship with your children, don't lose sight of your other relationships. If you're married or in a close relationship, set aside time for that relationship. The amount of time and what you do during it depend on your budget and what child care is available. The two of you could:

- talk together after the children are in bed

- take walks

- ride bikes or play a sport together (but leave time to talk)

- have a picnic

- go out to dinner

- get away for a weekend

During your special time together set aside thoughts of the children. Instead, focus on your relationship. Listen to each other, share feelings, encourage each other and *have fun together.*

And keep in touch with friends, whether they're other parents of young children, have older children or have no children. Even occasional phone calls will keep your friendship going.

What will you do this week with your partner? What will you do this week to maintain your friendships?

From: *Parenting Young Children* by Don Dinkmeyer et al. Circle Pines, MN: American Guidance Services, 1989. p. 64.

Learn More About It:

Dinkmeyer, Don and Jon Carlson. *Time for a Better Marriage.* Circle Pines, MN: American Guidance Services, 1984.
_____. *Taking Time for Love.* New York: Prentice Hall, 1989.
Fischer, Kathleen R. and Thomas N. Hart. *Promises to Keep: Developing the Skills of Marriage.* New York: Paulist Press, 1991.

4. ENCOURAGING YOUNG CHILDREN

Encouragement is a skill parents can learn to help children grow in self-esteem. Encouragement focuses on children's strengths and assets and recognizes their efforts and improvements. Unlike *comparing*, which measures children's worth by whether they do better or worse than others, *encouraging* reflections an appreciation for the child's unique qualities and abilities. Encouraging allows children to make internal evaluations, to decide for themselves if they are pleased with their efforts. Parents can offer children the encouragement needed to develop their inner resources and courage by:

- valuing and accepting children for who they are, with different abilities, interests, and rates of development;

- believing in children and showing it;

- treating children with respect;

- making it clear that a child's worth doesn't depend on being better than others;

- showing appreciation for children's efforts and improvements;

- appreciating children's strengths and positive qualities;

- showing real interest in areas that children find interesting and important;

- keeping a sense of humor that puts mistakes in perspective and allows children and their parents to relax.

Remember, from birth onward, children are forming beliefs about their self-worth. Treating children with respect and encouraging their attempts to grow enhance their sense of self-esteem. Encouragement doesn't demand perfection but sets reasonable goals, accepts children's efforts and appreciates their improvements.

[Adapted from: *Parenting Young Children* by Don Dinkmeyer et al. Circle Pines, MN: American Guidance Services, pp. 49-51.]

RESPONDING TO THOSE IN NEED AND RELATING TO THE WIDER COMMUNITY

Families respond to the gospel call to service by reaching out in compassion to those in need. This is done when:

- family members model the gospel values of respect for human dignity, compassion, justice and service to others in their relationships with each other and with others in the community;

- families learn about justice issues and the needs of others;

- family members participate together in parish and community service programs geared to their interests and abilities;

- families discuss how the needs of others, locally and globally, affect their life as a family;

- families join with others in society to alleviate the suffering of those in need and change the structures that allow injustice and inequality to continue.

Families work to better understand the world they live in and make it a better place for all people. This is done when:

- families model hospitality, opening their home to others, showing how God's love is communicated through family life;

- families grow in appreciation of their own ethnic or cultural heritage;

- families take part in parish and community events that help them understand the life and history of people of different cultures and nations and value cultural diversity as a special gift from God;

- families recognize their connectedness with and reliance upon others at all levels of life and grow in their appreciation for interdependence;

- families learn about and join in action with others who share a common vision and approach for improving life in the community.

The following activities provide examples of how families with preschool children can share the values of compassion and concern for others, and reach out together in response to the needs of the local and wider community.

1. SPECIAL DESSERT DAYS

Young children (like adults) like to eat and party. Special days in their lives are often tied up with special meals—and especially special desserts. Adding a few "special dessert days" to your family calendar can help your child(ren) connect with special days being celebrated by the wider community. On Earth Day serve large sugar cookies and tubes of colored frosting, inviting family members to decorate and celebrate their "planet." Celebrate ethnic or national holidays important to your family with special ethnic meals or desserts. Serve your breakfast eggs scrambled and green on St. Patrick's day (a little food coloring goes a long way!) or pumpkin soup (well-seasoned) and *grillot* (deep-fried pork) on Haitian Independence day. A memorable and celebrative meal, even for kids, makes the event equally memorable.

2. MOTHERING NATURE

O Lord, our God, your greatness is seen in all the world! (Psalm 8:1) Help young people to appreciate the beauty of nature and to understand our call from God to cherish it and care for it. Visit a city park or arboretum, or go for a slow-paced hike through the woods, attentive to the different sights and sounds, colors and textures. Try to view life from a two-, three-, or four-footer's perspective. Take time to see the small things and to touch almost everything. Give even a young child an easy-care plant of his or her own. Talk about what it needs to grow strong and our responsibility to help it grow. Start an egg carton of seeds on the window sill or help a cutting grow new roots. Appreciate the beauty. Talk about our responsibility to "mother" nature along.

3. TOYS AND VALUES

Playing is important "work" for young children. It helps children learn more about themselves and others, build their motor skills, solve simple problems and stretch their imaginations. Given the amount of time put into play, it is important that the toys they use reflect the values with which you want them to grow. Choose toys that reflect the values you hold, and let the other gift-sharers in your family know what kinds of toys you would like for your child. In developing a wish list for Christmas or birthday sharing, consider questions like the following:

- Do the toys, books, games and puzzles reflect an image of the world as a community of diverse and talented people?

- Do they provide opportunities to work together and model collaborative, rather than competitive, approaches to problem-solving?

- Do they help young children see that all people— women and men, blacks and whites, Americans and non-Americans—have similar potential, are capable of doing the same things or holding the same jobs?

4. TELLING A BOOK BY ITS COVER (AND CONTENT)

Reading can be a great way of opening young children's minds to fantasy worlds they have never before imagined—and of helping them cope with the very real world in which they are living. Recent years have seen a wonderful growth in the kinds of books written for young children. Make time when children are young to read to them regularly. As they get older, sit back and let them return the favor. Choose books that feature a variety of topics and settings. Select stories that help children to feel a variety of emotions and identify with a variety of people. Make sure the books, in their prose and in their illustrations, model a diversity of roles and a healthy respect for women and men, people of European descent and people of color, the young and the old.

Learn More About It:

McGinnis, Kathleen and Barbara Oehlberg. *Starting Out Right—Nurturing Children as Peacemakers.* St. Louis: The Institute for Peace and Justice, 1988.

4. TV AND VALUES

The same concerns and approaches mentioned above with toys and books carry over into the programs that children watch on television. Even a simple, ten-minute cartoon can speak volumes about justice issues, for example, about how people should solve differences, what everybody should have or what roles rightfully belong to women and men. Watch TV together at least once a week. Discuss what is real or unreal in the situations and solutions presented. Raise the values questions that grow out of the stories, letting your child know why you share or reject the values presented in the TV program (or commercial). Draw parallels between what is presented on TV and what is happening in the life of your family or community.

5. MULTICULTURAL CONNECTIONS: DEVELOPING AN APPRECIATION FOR DIVERSITY

Every young child is a living sensory sponge—taking into himself everything he sees, hears, tastes, smells and especially touches! Without realizing it, children begin, as well, to take in the values and messages that those around them attach to things. Slowly, what they sense in the home around them becomes the "norm" or acceptable thing. It is important, therefore, that the child's home is a place where diversity is present and appreciated. Toys, books and games can be chosen that make a conscious effort to include people of different racial and ethnic groups. Photos and artwork displayed around the home can be chosen with the same sensitivity to diversity. Using a Christmas creche that was made in El Salvador or an image of the Blessed Mother attired in Asian or African garb speaks volumes about God's concern for all people. When diversity is valued at home, it becomes much easier to value beyond the home as well.

Learn More About It:

The guides to children's reading suggested earlier in this chapter feature many books guaranteed to open children up to the wonder of different ethnic and national cultures.